This Is Are

Roma Beth Bonner

*To: Lisa and Tony,
friends for a divine
purpose...*

*Love,
Beth*

Copyright © 2014 Roma Beth Bonner

All rights reserved.

ISBN-13: 978-1496017925
ISBN-10: 1496017927

ACKNOWLEDGEMENTS

This book is dedicated to my beautiful little mother, Norma Lucille Davis Paulk, who is now in the great beyond with her precious Savior. My mother commissioned this book, she had a dream concerning it and shared it with me. She told me before she passed to "write the book, it's your message, don't worry about what others think, just do it". I think somehow she has played a very significant role in these writings from her new perspective!
I love you Mother, I did it!

I want to thank all of those who have played into my life. All of the men and women who believed in me through the years and poured into me, and the many who pray for me. To my Purple Butterfly Warrior community, I pray a blessing for you. I am thankful for my childhood friend who helped restore my faith in humanity, by listening to me, encouraging me, and very simply making me laugh. I want to thank those who have taken the time to invest in my life in any way. Truly, whatever role you have played has helped bring me here. I want to appreciate the ones who have taught me love, the ones who God let snuggle up next to me to give me the opportunity to learn either how to become vulnerable or learn how to let go. I can't say that this process has always been easy as I've had to let go of some who took a piece of my heart, the good thing is, I have given them all to God and thank Him for the good things they left with me and the lessons I've learned. I will be grateful Until the End of Time!!

And Finally, I want to thank my family, first my husband who knows who he is. He's never been one to feel threatened, he trusts me and it's taken his trust to shield me. Because every time I fell into his arms, he was there with understanding to pick me up. Wes Bonner, I would not want to have lived this journey with anyone else! From our first hardship of the flying roaches in our bedroom on our first night together in our house as newlyweds, through major battles of life and death you have stood by me and shielded me. Maybe not always like I thought you should, but obviously successfully. Thanks for putting up with this little girl's laughter and tears!

And to my children, you are truly the best God could have ever given us!! You are a reflection of God's love for me. Britt, you're still my rock, and Penielle, you continue to reveal God's beauty and wisdom to me daily. And my children by design, Cissy and Ryan, anyone who loves my children has my heart! Nine years ago God blessed me with my first grandchild...a part of me awoke with my Asher and my heart expanded, he has truly brought us blessings, I will always enjoy being a grandmother above all else. Ava, you're my Princess and Alston, what a miraculous little man! And soon to be, Ari, you will bring a new dimension of love into our lives. And to my brave sister, Joy, and all my extended family who are valiant and fight their own battles fearlessly, I love you. H, you know this Rosie can't say enough about your encouragement, love you!

Now to all my many spiritual children, Heads up! Mama's about to rock your world again! Love to all.

CONTENTS

Acknowledgements
Preface
Introduction
1 Let's Pour
2 What "Bride"?
3 Remembering Who You Are
4 The Shafts of Sacrifice
5 How we Cooperate with Love's Purpose
6 Preparing the "Now" place
7 Change or Bust!
8 The Tears of Sacrifice
9 The Decision to Expand and Build
10 The Bed
11 What a Beautiful Bed
12 Being Bedded
13 The Bed that Creates Life
14 The Newlywed Bed and the Writings of Love
15 Written by the Light
16 God's Fingers
17 Writing our Defense
18 Set the Table
19 Table Teamwork
20 Institution of the Lord's Supper
21 Sit Down and Set a Spell
22 Turn on the Lamp Please
23 The Room is Ready
24 Embrace Your Promise

PREFACE

If you are reading this book, perhaps you are one of the many who have been battling with our spiritual realities. Perhaps at one time you were devoted to a religion which, at the time, seemed to accommodate the quest of your spiritual man. Maybe you spent many years in the church system only to find yourself with even more questions about why you haven't found your place in the economy of God, or truly realized peace in your daily circumstances. Maybe you were even serving in a role in a religious organization and became disillusioned at seeing how the church, particularly the Christian Church, has become laden with a corporate mentality at the expense of caring for and leading people to a better understanding of God. Maybe you are just tired, tired of searching, seeking, asking, hoping and hurting only to be met with criticism from others or a very cryptic understanding of who this higher being is, if He really is, and how you came to be. Why are we really here and where are we going? I have lived my life from birth in the church, spending over twenty years listening to the questions that are forever eluding humanity. I have witnessed many "moves" of God, "revivals", spent my life in the study of God's Word teaching and ministering. I have been groomed to lead by some of the best, and lost myself in trying to achieve the goal of performing my best for God. I have Pastored a church of several hundred people, taking care of all the needs of the community, and loving them like my own. I have buried, married, prayed for, held the dying, held the newborn up to God in Holy consecration, ordained ministers and pastors, helped the widows and orphans and spent many years in the study of the bible. I have travelled for speaking engagements and to help churches in need, and to love the unlovable and forgive the unthinkable. I have seen the best and the worst of what the church has to say and offer. But here I am today after three years in a spiritual wilderness, having lost any semblance of a church, ministry or fellowship. Put on the side lines to write the things God has been showing me. It's the "manifestation of the sons of God" or the coming out of exile of a group of seekers, so hungry, yet sometimes so spiritually disoriented who I write to. It is those who really desire and ache to become who they are as God's child and are interested in finding the channel to release God's abilities in their lives and through their lives, this has become my passion. I have found that I am a motivator, and in motivating myself, I release the motivation God has given through me to others. That motivation is the force which leads people to an understanding of how to accept themselves as God does, how to be the best they can be for themselves and others, and how to identify and use their God created gifting to shine His love into the world, thereby healing it. The complexity of this life is simple, be who you are, where you are, all the time. There is a force to be released through humanity and how that force is to be released through you is entirely up to God and not you, all you have to do is mentally, spiritually, emotionally, and physically show up. But the least significant of these would be the location in which you physically show up. We are who we are wherever we are, this is almost so simple that it is rushed over in an attempt to make life about something more than it really is. In reaching my own "bottom" I learned how to let go of everything and everyone but myself and hold onto nothing but the fabric God gave me when He created me. I came naked into this world and I will leave this world naked. But not in my current identity. I was born, as you were, to fill up a space on this planet for a designated time, as a designated person, with a designated purpose, and a designated personality by which to accomplish a designated thing, this thing? To bring healing to this world, and be God's ambassador. The end goal? To provide an environment on this earth that is suitable for a God to come and dwell with us, and in doing so return this earth and all its inhabitants to its intended state.

But in order to reach any understanding and hope of a brighter day, we must all be willing to let go of our religious thought processes concerning "God". We cannot be afraid to step out from behind the excuses we've all made that keep us frozen into a form unusable to God. Excuses such as, "I got hurt, I don't trust, I've lost my desire, who am I to help people and how can I heal the earth when I myself am hurting and facing challenges and giants that keep me immobilized?" And those who have remained faithful in all they do, but yet know there's more? You are who God is calling. He is calling you to do unprecedented things, to come out from among them, to listen to the clarion call of the Spirit trying to wake us up into the knowledge of who and what we were made to be!! That group that the Word calls "the Bride". I'm going to not only show you the way out, that I was shown, but take you along on the journey with me to find a truth we can believe in and stake our lives upon. Hopefully by the time you've read through these writings, you yourself can simply take up where I leave off and write your own manuscript of your journey to true peace, joy, and serenity! I'm no one special in myself, but I know that in this earthen vessel lies a secret to everything I need to live this life in a fresh way and with total and complete fulfillment. And I'm alive to share it.

Introduction

It begins with this invaluable scripture, *"The God who made the world and everything in it, this Master of sky and land, doesn't live in custom–made shrines or need the human race to run errands for him, as if he couldn't take care of himself. He makes the creatures; the creatures don't make him. Starting from scratch, he made the entire human race and made the earth hospitable, with plenty of time and space for living so we could seek after God, and not just grope around in the dark but actually find him. He doesn't play hide–and–seek with us. He's not remote; he's near. We live and move in him, can't get away from him!"*
Acts 17:24-28 MSG

What an elemental and necessary understanding of how life works, how we work, upon which everything exists. If you don't believe there is a Divine or higher force responsible for all that's seen, then you can stop here and take your chances at a meaningful life. But it's evident by the study of the human condition that those who believe in a higher purpose, and a Divine force responsible for our existence, are much better equipped and mentally capable to cope within the limitations of what we know as the human existence. But if you, like me, are a seeker who desires to live life at the highest possible level of understanding, which gives hope, then reading on will encourage you at the least and inspire you at the most to make a true difference wherever you are with no limitations!

1 LET'S POUR

Having been married to a home builder for 36 years has equipped me with the knowledge of how a home is constructed from the ground up. The very first and most important thing, which remains the most important thing for the life of the house, is how the foundation was prepped and poured. Much care must be taken at this point because the rest of the home's endurance and integrity rests upon it. If the foundation is cracked or weakened initially, eventually it will show up, compromising the whole structure. I can't tell you how many times I've heard him say "we're gonna pour today!" I always know that is a jam packed statement meaning many things. It is the culmination of circumstances beyond his control, like weather, subs, available concrete, inspections, permits and the proper scheduling. It is the proclamation that victory is around the corner and soon a beautiful home will rise from the ground! In that reality, we start where we must in order to provide the builder with a thorough foundation that when inspected by the the Holy Spirit, is fit for his use. So we start first with foundational truths which are imperative.

First, we began by understanding that there is so much truth in the scripture that simply says, "Be still and know that I am God". The very first absolute that we must recognize in establishing a firm foundation is that there is a "God" an invisible force by which we all operate. Each and every cell of our body moves to an invisible rhythm, if separated from its purpose or the other cells that it cooperates with in doing its job, it ceases to function and the cell dies. It is scientifically documented that there is no explanation as to why, say, a heart cell, will only function as a heart cell, but we know that this is true and we see that we, even though comprised of those cells, have no power over how long or how hard those cells continue to work together. But as long as they cooperate, they are accomplishing their purpose by pumping life's blood. We are all constructed, if you will, from materials that respond in symphony to this invisible force, the force we best know as "love". It is the fuel for the existence of humanity, the whole fabric of space and time, everything we know and don't know is made from a fabric that only shows up off of the backdrop or setting of this love. The fibers of this fabric of everything are brought into visibility as light shines upon them. Even as the human eye is made with the capacity to reflect images off of light, so is this fabric seen cosmically, and on a greater divine scale, when it is illuminated by the light it was created to reflect. It is so imperative to understand how we as flesh beings, implanted with invisible qualities of these fibers are created to show forth the light...who is God. The truth is we can't help but shine if we are in the light no more than a mirror can stop from reflecting sunlight on a bright sunny day. We were made by a divine force with fabric that is illuminated only when we put it in the environment that holds the key to it's illumination. It just so happens that the environment in which it shines is given inertia by the fuel of love, which in simple terms, is God.

But Love can do nothing in a vacuum by virtue of the truth that love GIVES. If their is no object of affection on which to bestow love, there is no such thing as love. So this God or "Love", for His own reasons that only He and Himself knew, made the decision to create a love interest. His love interest then became His creation.

So now we introduce what the whole point of creation is and the expected end...this is the foundation to finding all the answers every human being seeks...

"I, John, saw the holy city, New Jerusalem, coming down out of heaven from God, prepared as a bride adorned for her husband. And I heard a loud voice from heaven saying, "Behold, the tabernacle of God is with men, and He will dwell with them, and they shall be His people. God Himself will be with them and be their God. And God will wipe away every tear from their eyes; there shall be no more death, nor sorrow, nor crying. There shall be no more pain, for the former things have passed away."
Rev 21:2-4 NKJV

It was very kind of God to show us our destiny. No man having read this passage can say that they don't know man's destiny or their own personal destiny. This Revelation received by John on the Isle of Patmos was given to reveal our destiny and a summary of the culmination of things to come. I don't know about you, but every time I read this, it gives me peace. This book of the bible gives us such a chaotic and violent view of the end of time...as we know it. It won't be the end of time as God knows it, for He never ends, and we will be in Him for eternity, whatever that means, and no one can literally say they know what that means except those who now view it from an eternal vantage point.

We were created to have light and love reflected from us...and to be companionship for a God beyond our understanding and no other relationship on planet earth describes this kind of relationship better than a husband and wife. So it is our destiny to go back into God to be his beloved. I don't know about you, but I can live with that! It doesn't matter what I'm doing, it's who I am reflecting, who I am BEING.

Continuing along those lines, and filtering everything through this fundamental concept, we can see how we have been told for thousands of years and even longer where time and eternity is taking us and the destiny that lies before the human race. We are building towards something and in order to get there we must drop all the pretense we have built up about ourselves over centuries and be willing to go back to the simplest of thinking, even as like a child. None of the world's greatest minds, not Einstein, or Hawkings, none of the "great" minds have had all of the truth for only pieces are being revealed as they are illuminated to us. Why? We ask, well that's all part of the equation, that we simply trust that what works in us daily without any effort on our part, is ultimately that thing that will drive us to our destiny. We don't ask why internally or biologically, we are having to inhale oxygen in order to fill up our lungs that in turn oxygenates the blood. The life giving blood that flows into our organs, giving them life with the nutrients it provides, thus making us function as a human being. It just happens. Am I espousing that we have no responsibility as members of the human race as to how this whole thing culminates or as to the effect we can have on outcomes and consequences? No, as we can clearly see, nothing is illuminated without a source of illumination, and here is where we begin to understand that our responsibility merely has to do with what we don't do as opposed to what we actually do.

We are already created and naturally given the nature of the Divine, our creator and yes, we have it within our framework to also demonstrate and function on a baser level. We are all born with DNA which we now know is the strain upon which our lives are constructed, and this DNA predisposes us to respond and behave a certain way. Beginning with the fall of man away from the God nature, this DNA has taken on a pattern more representative of an animalistic, or carnal and mere mortal nature than it's beginning at creation. At creation most religions and theologians insert a garden... a garden is indicative of where life begins from the dirt. Anyone knows, especially those in the agricultural fields, that without "soil" or "dirt", "terra- firma", nothing can grow. And each individual culture, religious sect, tribe, and people groups have their own variety or translation of what or where this has it's beginnings. But the fact is that there is definitely a place of origin where life began, whether, as the scientific community theorizes it was a "big bang" or as the Christian culture holds fast that it was an actual place, and specific time at which God created man, the fact is we have become who we are. If indeed, we were created from the explosion of light which we will call "love", then it was still the handy work of a greater force than any of us can comprehend or explain. All we need do is "recognize" this explosive force...which began the process we are still cooperating in, either willingly or unwillingly. Two key words here are "recognize" and "cooperate".

Before we can understand our becoming process as children of this force of life or "God" as we call it, we must recognize it. We must acknowledge not only with our minds but also with our hearts with the invisible portion of life, which we know as our "spirit" nature, that we are not responsible for anything this force did not create. In truth, we are not the highest form of life and we aren't actually making anything happen. That said, we arrive at "cooperation". What we are doing is cooperating in a plan set in motion for purposes beyond our comprehension, try as we may to explain it, we can't, but we can work in cooperation with it. In doing this we live a fulfilled life, joyful, and even happy because we began to assume the position we were made to assume as a vessel containing something packed inside our spiritual DNA or "fabric" and this is calling us to the ever higher task of just "being". This is how we will become the manifestation of God, by reflecting Him in truth to this world and not just in part. We recognize our dependency upon the force of life called "love" which is activated by a response to that light that is shining upon us. And it shines without our help, but with our cooperation, then we can become reflectors and illuminators ourselves bringing more of the Divine into this realm and upon this earth. In so doing we become the sons of God and something critical happens. This critical happening has also been depicted as a great battle between good and evil, or as the coming of God's authority on this planet in the form of Christ or His Body, or as life in an alternate reality we would call "heaven". Whatever we perceive as the eternal state of the human race or even the planet is where we see everything culminating. And my desire as a daughter of vision, birthed through much trial and error, pain and persecution, loss and hard lessons, is to simply share some insights on how we can assume a position in life to best cooperate with our Creator and His Creation. That we might live a life not burdened with the egotistical philosophy of living to do something great, but of just "being", and in so doing, multiplying greatness. A greatness beyond which no one person could ever achieve by living life simply unto himself trying to leave a "mark" or make a "name" for himself. We should be aware that all names will diminish into one of two eventually, either life, or death...darkness or light, brighter or flickered out into smoke that dissipates into nothingness. I am proposing here that if you are reading this book, it is your time to shine. I am cooperating in this flow by sharing these truths that were deposited within me for my personal growth and to share with seekers everywhere. Those who desire to be contributing to the betterment of the world as well as the betterment of their own condition. Isn't that all of us?

So in essence these thoughts should lead us into the understanding of a truth shared in scripture about the time for the "manifestation" of the sons of God. The coming down of the "Holy City", the revealing of the "New Jerusalem",the "Bride of Christ.

2 WHAT "BRIDE"?

There is a complete yet complex paradigm shift when we begin to look out beyond ourselves in recognition of the need for a divine source of reflection. Christianity has always embraced the teaching of Christ as Him being the "light of the world", but it's been thrown around in such generalities that it has become just another watered down saying convoluted into the mix of many of Jesus' other parables and teachings. However, the concept itself is truly a phenomenal truth when we become open, shedding ourselves of preconceptions about what He meant. There is no shortage of scriptures concerning the Divine light which comprises the backdrop off of which everything else stands. In the first book of the Bible, the Genesis, where Moses tells us how the whole of creation began, we are told that God, the life force, spoke and said "let there be light". He created without light according to Genesis, He created everything at the same time, that which is seen, the evident, and that which is not seen, which conveys to us the truth that there is a realm, if you will, not visible to the human eye. But that doesn't mean it wasn't created and it doesn't mean we have no way of seeing into it. We see the weightiness of this realm in the following passage:

"Therefore we do not lose heart. Even though our outward man is perishing, yet the inward man is being renewed day by

day. For our light affliction, which is but for a moment, is working for us a far more exceeding and eternal weight of glory, while we do not look at the things which are seen, but at the things which are not seen. For the things which are seen are temporary, but the things which are not seen are eternal."
2 Cor. 4:17-18 NKJV

In order to see into the invisible realm, we are given a fire that will lead the way, we also know this guide or aid as the "Holy Spirit" who was sent by Jesus after He had ascended back to God once His job of "manifesting" or showing this light was accomplished. But He made it abundantly clear the purposes for which He would send this new power to assist those who believed in Him, and It was to equip them with power for the purpose of the witnessing of His message. Which is just another way of saying "I am going to send the fire to illuminate you, to shine upon the truth I have deposited inside each of you". "Witness" means to be seen or to "reveal" or "show forth". In other words, we would "shed light" as vessels of this truth of who the Christ is, and in turn the Power that backed Him. And this is the good news of a God who is the love force, the force that produces life. He instructed the disciples to go and wait at a particular location, and they cooperated, which put them in the proper place to become illuminated. This experience is described in the book of Acts as beginning, of course, with just a group of 120 people in an upstairs room. They were simply waiting in anticipation of something they had been promised and believed to be true. This coming of the Spirit that Jesus had foretold could look or sound like anything. Having been around Him and witnessed His style of teaching and illustrating, they most probably had already formed somewhat of an opinion as to what this coming Spirit might appear as, or sound like, or do when it got there. But what fascinates me is that it started as an element of nature, a wind, and why would we be surprised? God is nature, as we saw in Genesis He made every bit of this world we know and all the "elements" known to it. Therefore in this instance, He even says that He will send this "force" to these people. First as a rushing mighty wind, but eventually the "illumination" arrived in the form of cloven tongues of fire which would probably look something like columns or rays of light being dispensed to each individual. And let me note that He speaks of this force as a guide into all truth, this force of the Holy Spirit illuminates us in all things but particularly in our everyday walk of life. A side note of truth at this point is that just as these disciples and followers of Christ were expectant without knowing exactly what would happen, so are we. We, the spiritual seekers, are poised on the brink of the most exciting time in human history, when our mission here is completed and Christ literally returns as He promised. Because His methods always outwit ours and because we are limited in understanding beyond this realm, we don't really know what we are looking for. The only way to identify the end of this time period, as we've known it is by the signs we are given in scripture. The scripture talks about God's Word being a lamp unto my feet and a light unto my path. Whenever light is being addressed in God's contexts it is usually referring to a form of guidance.

Could it be then that as Jesus was and is the light of the world, and as He shines and illuminates from within us that not only will our paths be clear, just naturally, but wherever we go "manifesting" this light the residual affect will be to cause others to more clearly see what truly surrounds them on their path? In the scripture Jesus uses the term "the Kingdom of God" quite often! And when He does He is not describing a particular dispensation, or time period. He is actually describing the realm we cannot see, but in which we find our purpose. When we step into the designed blue print for this Universe, life, love, and creation in general, we are being governed by the realm where God rules. It's from this dimension that we draw our spiritual life's blood. There are many in-depth truths to be revealed here about this "Kingdom of God" dimension, but for the purposes of our journey here, we will simply use it in a generalization describing wherever God is, and where He is, He is sovereign.

In the church world, a common metaphor used quite often is that as dark grows darker, the light will grow brighter. Well why not? Is it not in the darkest of hours that any form of light seems so much brighter popping off that dark background? I believe now is the the time and will become even more so for the sons of God to begin to shine brighter and brighter, not necessarily for anything we've done on our parts, but because the days in which we live seem to be gaining darkness with speed and intensity. What I am having revealed to me as more and more people come to me asking "where's my ministry? What's my place?" Is that it's not at all about seeking for where and what we are to do, but who we are to be wherever we are. It astounds me at the people who still believe in order to make a difference for good, and be an influence as a Christ thinker, they must play some grand role in the organized church. This is not so and if anything, those in the positions of carrying on a work from an organized place of worship have a much harder time being bright enough to really show forth the "energeo" spoken of in the bible. It's when forces of darkness emerge, which seems to be the prevailing trend, that we make more headway.

We have such a strung out and misunderstood view of what the Church of our Lord Jesus Christ is to be that we have lost sight of where it really is. We, the "Christ minded followers" are each the church, we are His temple, but a loose definition of church is "the gathering of souls, or an assembly". I'm in no way negating the role churches play in our culture in America and in our society, I'm challenging anyone who calls themselves a "believer" to rethink what and who the church really is and what it is "becoming"! It is a living organism, therefore, its growth and evolution is literally unstoppable. It's very easy to get stuck in a concept that leads us nowhere but traps us inside old customs and rituals. This is not the "Kingdom" described in God's word. It has little or nothing to do with the limitations we place upon ourselves for religious sanctity, it is more a state of "being". Christ better describes His Church as "His Body", in this world being a living organism which changes matures and functions in the world as He did.

Let's look it square in the face and call it what it is, most of our church Institutions are merely hospitals, nurseries, and social mechanisms for the believing Christian. A place to go lick our wounds, gain strength by sharing truths and sharing in a corporate attitude of worship that gives us validation in all we feel and do. There are things that transpire in an assembly that cannot happen on a personal level, I think we can all agree on that. There are some churches who strive to be more apostolic, looking at the whole world as their assembly, and there are those who operate more evangelistically, viewing the outside world as a field to be harvested. And then there are those who spend the greatest energy helping God do His business of training His children, equipping them for service, and keeping them strengthened. All of these hold an evident truth and a valid place. However all of these various church types are diminishing, what is becoming more evident are those believers inside the institution and outside who are beginning to grasp the concept that the new era we have entered is not about where we attend church or who mentors us or what we say and do. It's becoming about being who we are as a son or daughter of the force of life, creation, and the resurrection we find demonstrated through Christ, wherever we go. I'm not arguing about the validity of the church, anything that helps make us shine brighter and brings more of that light into one place can't be bad, but the real call to ministry is not in or about church, it's about "being" the church and finding our true identity within this realm of reality as "the Bride", the manifest sons of God. "Manifest" being the imperative frame of reference. The only way history will culminate in victory for humanity is if and when we come out of our isolating "churches" of thoughts and patterns and begin to have a knowledge in ourselves of the higher purpose we were made for and called to.

Incidentally, what I am writing about is in no way a new concept. The great Fathers and Mothers of the faith have been leading us into this for many decades. Each, having their own role to play and their messages to espouse, but now the Work of God is becoming fine tuned inside the lives of those with yearning hearts and listening ears. Each of us is becoming aware of what resides within us and has from the beginning of time. Christ stepped off the time line of what we define as past present and future and became the instrument whereby God, or divine love, could illustrate to us our created capabilities and help light the way into the destiny we must now assume. Those who are progressively Christ minded, following the "proceeding" Word of God, not just from pages that can be cut apart, dissected, used, misrepresented, and twisted, but from within themselves as they surrender to the divine interpretation of God's love within us all, these are they who will live out a purpose far greater than any generation, society, or culture has ever realized before! These are His Bride!

3 REMEMBERING WHO YOU ARE

There has been a trend in recent years of a surge of people avoiding religious institutions. Most of these people have not lost their desire to know God or to stay alive in their spiritual awareness and journey. They sense themselves growing and feel almost as if the church as an institution, generalizing here, limits their ability to begin transforming into the liberty of living out their predestined purpose of reflecting pure radiance and love. They find comfort in listening and learning from spiritual teachers who lead in the ways of love. These are they who are not denying Christ, just the organizations which depict Him in ways contrary to his redemptive essence. Jesus Christ was all about acceptance, peace, righteousness (or living according to love's standard) and joy, or the knowing with confidence that we are sheltered in His love. Many of these feel they have escaped the limitations placed on them, not by the Word, but by men's interpretation of it. The failure of many insensitive religious leaders and the scars perpetrated against many (whether genuine or perceived) have pushed them into a position to seek something genuine in their minds. Even though being led by the Spirit is paramount to their growth, they have lost touch with the institution of men's making and moved towards the Christ of the Word. In an attempt not to cast judgment upon them or negate any religious organization, just let me say I believe in a community of love. I know the necessity and benefits of gathering together as God's people in an organized assembly, and the need for teachers, preachers and care givers. But there is no denying that changes are taking place within the hearts of all men to take personal responsibility as temples of God's Spirit. Gone are the days of seekers depending solely upon learned and gifted men and women for their own spiritual growth and understanding. Mature leadership in any situation discerns this and allows for this, not compromising the standard of Christ's example, but allowing everything to only compliment that. These different components provided for our growth should be able to work in conjunction with one another and run parallel in our lives, leading us ultimately to the zenith of our existence. If one is pulling against the other, there can be a great struggle not only within the individual believer, but the residual fall out can destroy churches and good people of God. There is a cry for truth, mercy, and spiritual evolution to walk arm in arm leading us to new places and deeper fulfillment. In order to truly manifest as God's chosen, who have truly returned to love's first order, we must be willing to break down any barriers that we feel protect our beliefs or concepts.

Let's continue this process in our minds and hearts and see if we might better understand who we really are here and now, and how this leads us to the wedding feast at the end of time. This is where it begins:

"Since God has so generously let us in on what He is doing, we're not about to throw up our hands and walk off the job just because we run into occasional hard times. We refuse to wear masks and play games. We don't maneuver and manipulate behind the scenes. And we don't twist God's Word to suit ourselves. Rather, we keep everything we do and say out in the open, the whole truth on display, so that those who want to can see and judge for themselves in the presence of God.

If our Message is obscure to anyone, it's not because we're holding back in any way. No, it's because these other people are looking or going the wrong way and refuse to give it serious attention. All they have eyes for is the fashionable god of darkness. They think he can give them what they want, and that they won't have to bother believing a Truth they can't see.

They're stone-blind to the dayspring brightness of the Message that shines with Christ, who gives us the best picture of God we'll ever get. Remember our Message is not about ourselves; we're proclaiming Jesus Christ, the Master. All we are is messengers, errand runners from Jesus for you. It started when God said, "Light up the darkness!" and our lives filled up with light as we saw and understood God in the face of Christ, all bright and beautiful."
2 Corinthians 4:3-6 MSG

What a beautifully written passage, using the "Message" version we read the meaningfully crafted words Paul employed to show us Whose we are and who we are. This "dayspring brightness of the message that shines with Christ" is displayed off of this pre-eminent atmosphere, this shining message of love, where we can be seen, and this passage clearly reveals a very clever plan that God, as the force of love, devised to get the attention of all humanity for the purposes of restoration and recovery. In a rather sad scenario, the light was obscured by the failure of man to respond to it appropriately as the one Divine purpose for light. This was a side effect of mankind choosing rather to follow the course of his own carnal nature. This choice was and is simply the illusion crafted by man's own ego for self promotion. So Love had to find a way to reintroduce itself into an opposing world ruled no longer by the rhythm of love from which it was created, but confined by a darkness that had been spreading since the rejection of light, not long after creation. We are given the understanding that after this primary rejection of the light, usually having taken place in sequence with the garden of creation, that subsequent generations were born into this darkness not having had the opportunity to make the choice for themselves, they were now being born into a fallen or darkened plane of creation. And of course this put God's most beloved creation at a major disadvantage. Love, or God, refused to lose the object of His affection, which included mankind, and all other created things...even the terra-firma, or the very planet. for these things came about as the very expression of who God is... the very thing that defined Him as "love". Even as He had limited His own control by endorsing and creating the gift of "free will" in humanity, now He had to find a way to redeem or restore to light this love expression in a way that the generations now spawned in darkness could cooperate with. Some new scientific thought presents the possibility that as creatures of the earth, perhaps we have no "free will" at all. The way it has been presented would further promote the misconception that we are no more than a pawn in this huge universe playing out a role we aren't even aware of. But if that is true, what is driving us? What holds everything together and functioning as it should? It's like the law of gravity. We all take for granted that as long as gravity exists, we will not fall off of this planet, as Sir Isaac Newton observed. We operate inside of a gravitational pull not visible to us, but proven to exist by its very own properties, proven by the result it achieves. So if there is a force that we can't see governing our free will, which is directly contrary to most religious trains of thought, wouldn't there be some form of proof by which it could be identified? This argument is one left better unrealized since there is no proof that such a force exists. But, we know love exists, you can see it's fruit. Anything that shows itself, not just in theory, but in reality, exists. The fruit or the product is the evidence of the thing that is producing.

But we were limited because we, as His creation had lived in this darkness for so long, our "God eyes" that we possessed at creation had now become dim, not allowing us to see things how they really are. Just as the first man and woman we are told, began to see themselves no longer as a divine reflection of their creator, they became hidden in their own shame, perceiving through this veil of darkness that their own created bodies were unclean. As time and generations progressed and evolved, man simply had begun to adapt to the environment in which we now existed...just as any God given skill or ability will diminish without proper use...so our spiritual eyes which perceive this divine light, had begun to be dulled and even blinded. God recognized at this point that He had to begin immediately providing portals of rediscovery for us through various shafts of illumination.

4 THE SHAFTS OF SACRIFICE

The Old testament recounts for us many of these "shafts", which sometimes manifested in the form of people, and sometimes in circumstances. But none of these plans held enough sway to keep darkness from ebbing back in. So, finally God, as love, made the decision to return Himself into this hostile environment, but He purposed to do it in a way so that the already fragile creation could best receive Him and not be blinded again. it would take a major sacrifice for love to do His work. (Side note...it's only in this redemptive ebb and flow that seekers can be restored and recovered.)

But the sacrifice was not without return in that as He lavished His love upon His own creation, He was setting up the total plan and provision for His light to be dispersed through many vessels and eventually be so prolific that it multiplied the intensity of who He really is. This could then be seen through the many who would respond to this love and become heirs and joint heirs in this plan to redeem and reclaim a lost creation. The Old Testament recounts to us many instances in which a man or group of people were challenged to sacrifice something of great earthly value so that the place left empty and standing could be refilled with something better and even life giving. One example would be the example of the ultimate sacrifice when Abraham was asked to take his son Isaac up to the mountain of sacrifice and lay him on the alter there. This son given to Isaac, had been so long awaited and in revisiting the story we see that Isaac had been a gift from God into an otherwise impossible situation of barrenness and old age. It would then seem cruel of a God who gave this life, to reclaim it in the form of a brutal slaying, which was unavoidable in the Israelite culture. It was laid out specifically for them how a sacrifice was to be prepared and slaughtered, in their own written concepts of the law. Therefore if Abraham were to sacrifice this son he could not do it in a way as to spare his son the discomfort of knowing what was immediately at hand. This young boy, who had so innocently and trustingly followed his father up a mountain slope to participate in giving a sacrifice to God, now became the object of sacrifice. Would it have otherwise been a sacrifice? One must question the authenticity of a sacrifice if indeed there is no pain associated with it. It's in the giving up that we find the pain, but it is in the refilling that we find the gain. Once Abraham demonstrated his desire to make a place for God to refill, it became evident that the Author of life had something else in mind altogether, and it was proven to Abraham that after the journey to the sacrifice has been made and the carnal will rejected, which is always a painful exercise, God will show up with the real substance. He'll show up, not only with something else for us to lay before Him in an attitude of gratefulness, but also a new revelation about who "He" is. God did, in this story, provide a lamb in the thicket for the purposes of showing His pleasure with Abraham's willing demeanor and attitude...so what had before been a mandate given to Abraham to sacrifice his own precious son, now becomes an opportunity to mentor the next generation in how sacrifice is a heart issue and not necessarily concerned with the value of the actual sacrifice.

In this scenario Abraham deemed it necessary to not take any other kind of sacrifice with him up the mountain and to the altar because of His confidence in the God who had shown Himself faithful to him by giving the boy Isaac as an heir that otherwise Abraham could never have. Abraham is a total and complete reflection of the Father of creation being willing to sacrifice His own dear son in an attempt to restore the world, the earth, and his creation, back to it's originally created state as a love story. A story in which there was a being who took notice of something null and void, a space that needed the attention of love, that needed to be nurtured and renewed. And something prompted Him to be move upon and that love begin to produce. He began speaking forth what this chaotic space needed in order to be adequate and capable of housing His divine nature. He began to spin out the very fabric of creation, and His first course of action was to speak forth light. To illuminate the truth of who love is. And as this light peeled back the inky black encasement that imprisoned unspoken possibilities, He formed and molded His most sacred and precious temple which He would call "man". He carefully formed this vessel in the image of how He viewed Himself to be and then sealed this earthen object with a seal of approval by giving it His very life's breath, His divine, supernatural, unlimited breath. We conclude that this created place was to also be capable of facilitating His presence since He desired to come and walk among His own created kind and spend time in fellowship. He could then naturally dwell among His created beauty and even delight in seeing these extraordinary vessels shed light into their own world, by helping Him illuminate the remainder of created substance by giving it names and calling it forth. What ultimately separated God from His own creation, and the ability to coexist peacefully within His own boundaries, was when man stepped out of his designated place as the "created" and began to want to circumvent the Creator's desire for simple pure expressed love. So by the time God had made His decision to come back Himself in the form of a man, He knew that it would require the necessary sacrifice, the giving up of His own life, so that the object of His affection not only could once again experience this divine love, but so that He could relight man's darkened existence by sharing the illumination of truth reflected in the face of Jesus.

Here it is plain and simple:

"All they have eyes for is the fashionable god of darkness. They think he can give them what they want, and that they won't have to bother believing a Truth they can't see. They're stone–blind to the dayspring brightness of the message that shines with Christ, who gives us the best picture of God we'll ever get. Remember, our Message is not about ourselves;

we're proclaiming Jesus Christ, the Master. All we are is messengers, errand runners from Jesus for you. It started when God said, "Light up the darkness!" and our lives filled up with light as we saw and understood God in the face of Christ, all bright and beautiful."
2 Corinthians 4:4-6 MSG

And this is where we take up, we are the many sons, we are called joint heirs, and God had to give us the Christ example and then send back the force Christ possessed, the force of light in truth and life in resurrection to equip us to finish the task. Now we have been reclaimed by our lover and are helping Him to reclaim His own. And we are vessels made for this honor.

5 HOW WE COOPERATE WITH LOVE'S PURPOSE

How then, knowing this, can we apply it in our daily, very limited existence and ensure our place in God's great plan? Yes, we know the end and we know we were all created to be God's Bride at the end, but how does the "free will" we were given at the onset of life fit into this divine formula? Simply put, we have a job to do, that is to be love's emissaries and missionaries on this strange planet. We are housed in temples that make it conducive for us to inhabit the hostility of this environment for a reason. How we respond to the Divine light will determine our status as we step into the next dimension with Love. For those of us who follow Christ, we believe our security in this to be found in accepting Jesus as God's Son and by following his instruction and example. These instructions and examples are interpreted very differently in various sects of "Christianity", but what I speak to in this book has nothing to do with abiding by laws or conduct, the very truth of it lies within us. In the part of us where God deposited His own Spirit. The part we cannot begin to tap into without the roadmap and a supernatural force to guide us, because for the living, it is unknown territory. But we must have a desire in our "Sozo" or inner core of our being to begin now with the intent of becoming the sons of God here...and the Bride of Christ for eternity.

In order to do this we must simply accept and cooperate with God's plan. We strive entirely too much with this and allow ourselves to be pulled off course. We "miss the mark". As Paul said, we must:

"lay aside every weight, and the sin which so easily ensnares us, and let us run with endurance the race that is set before us, looking unto Jesus, the author and finisher of our faith, who for the joy that was set before Him endured the cross, despising the shame, and has sat down at the right hand of the throne of God."
Heb 12:1-2 NKJV

And we will be seated right beside Him, but there are things we can and should be doing to hasten the day. This is a principle set forth by God himself when He instructed us to "draw nigh to God" and "seek first the Kingdom" among other exhortations. It's really our move and all of creation waits on us to begin to be uncovered, revealed and seen as the Sons and Daughters of God. So what can we do in our own lives to ensure we are evolving into a true divine force progressing God's ultimate plan?

Ask the Leading Lady

There is a woman we will look at who gives us a thorough insight into how to be fulfilled and continue in the direction of our own destiny. It is the story of the woman who longed for something so badly that she found a way to apprehend the man of God in her area and a different kind of sacrifice took place, one she was not prepared for or could even think possible:

"One day Elisha passed through Shunem. A leading lady of the town talked him into stopping for a meal. And then it became his custom: Whenever he passed through, he stopped by for a meal.
"I'm certain," said the woman to her husband, "that this man who stops by with us all the time is a holy man of God. Why don't we add on a small room upstairs and furnish it with a bed and desk, chair and lamp, so that when he comes by he can

stay with us?" And so it happened that the next time Elisha came by he went to the room and lay down for a nap. Then he said to his servant Gehazi, "Tell the Shunammite woman I want to see her." He called her and she came to him. Through Gehazi Elisha said, "You've gone far beyond the call of duty in taking care of us; what can we do for you? Do you have a request we can bring to the king or to the commander of the army?"
She replied, "Nothing. I'm secure and satisfied in my family." Elisha conferred with Gehazi: "There's got to be something we can do for her. But what?"
Gehazi said, "Well, she has no son, and her husband is an old man."
"Call her in," said Elisha. He called her and she stood at the open door.
Elisha said to her, "This time next year you're going to be nursing an infant son."
"O my master, O Holy Man," she said, "don't play games with me, teasing me with such fantasies!"

The woman conceived. A year later, just as Elisha had said, she had a son."
2 Kings 4:8-17 NKJV

Have you ever found yourself in the position of doubting the blessings that God is sending into your life because either you're afraid they'll be snatched away? Or, you are doubting that you are good enough to receive such grace? We don't receive necessarily based on our actions, but on our attitude. Two people can be going for the same job position, one is vehement that they are the one who will stride in and apprehend the job, the other is confident, but confident in his belief that God will give him the best for his journey. Look at it, if the man confident in his own abilities looses the job...he feels demeaned and diminished. But if the man who has his confidence in the God of love who rules the Universe doesn't get the position, he knows that God has prepared a better job down the road. To God time is nothing and actually one continual loop. Tomorrow is as good as today for the blessing, because whenever it is it will be on time! One could contend that all things happen simultaneously with God because there is no past, present, or future. A day is like a thousand years. And a blessing is a blessing, we are the ones with the time constraints. How can we as mere mortals bring comprehension to a truth so far beyond the synapses of our brains!? These brains, along with our bodies will return to dust...but what inhabited that bulk of changing cells called "you", that's what knows no time. The "you" created in the image of God, and God is not dirt, He is spirit and light. The "you" people see when they look into your eyes. When someone dies we say, "the light went out of their eyes", and its not just a saying, I have witnessed this many times. That's because what reflects from our eyes is the light of God, the true eternal flame! One can also see darkness in the eyes of those who have no light in them, they already look lifeless.

The written Word says that "the eyes are the windows to the soul". Here is what is said to give a better understanding:

"Brethren, I write no new commandment to you, but an old commandment which you have had from the beginning. The old commandment is the word which you heard from the beginning. Again, a new commandment I write to you, which thing is true in Him and in you, because the darkness is passing away, and the true light is already shining. He who says he is in the light, and hates his brother, is in darkness until now. He who loves his brother abides in the light, and there is no cause for stumbling in him. But he who hates his brother is in darkness and walks in darkness, and does not know where he is going, because the darkness has blinded his eyes."
1 Jn 2:7-11 NKJV

Doesn't it say something that this passage brings up that the amount of light we are able show forth is directly proportional to the amount of love we have for a brother?

Light and love are interchangeable. But there's no time like the present to understand who "you" really are because the only true moment we can be sure of is now, this moment in which you are reading these words. The divine source of your life never intended on you building up your confidence by the things He's blessed you with...houses, lands. I know it seems like something we hear constantly, but we can't hear it enough. Your life is not comprised of what you have, your life is a compilation of who and whose you are. Hundreds, thousands of years have helped bring people together to bond their DNA to form you for this moment, whatever age you are you are still in this dimension of life for a higher purpose than you can know. All you can do is follow where the daily path of enlightenment and love lead you. So, the man who went into get the job with the knowledge of whose he really was, the man who doesn't trust his own works and abilities wins no matter the outcome because it doesn't matter what he loses, he possesses his own life in God and no one can snatch that from him! However, the man who loses his own confidence because it has been misplaced in himself looses, no matter the outcome.

This story I'm referencing concerning the Shunammite woman and Elisha is just the beginning of a story rife with contradictions and misrepresentations. Yet, it brings a truth of what this life, life on this planet in a hostile environment for us, who were made as agents to be filled with light and love can sometimes present to us. And it's given in order to empty us, time and time again, to make room for more of this love we are destined to display.

6 PREPARING THE "NOW" PLACE

Emptying to make room

As the story in 2 Kings unfolds perhaps we can draw from it a divine perspective I speak of concerning sacrifice. This woman illustrates the principle of becoming a shaft of light. The prophet, considered to be God's very voice and representative on planet earth for this time in this culture's history, frequently travels through this city, Shunem. For whatever reason, he is being sent on a mission and he runs into an important Lady who obviously holds some ability to be persuasive, as she is able to convince this man of God to stop by her place for dinner. It seems from the story that we are given, that she has no ulterior motive other than simply to make a provision, or provide a room whereby this man could be refreshed. She doesn't ask for anything in return only makes the suggestion to her husband that they make an addition to their home to accommodate God's messenger. She has no ulterior motive other than simply to create a space which could be used in service to God as she understood Him. In doing this it opened up the possibility in God for her to receive something she didn't even know she needed. This is an example of how often times we think we know what we need from God and begin going hard after our desires instead of simply making more space in our own lives for divine possibilities we've never even explored. It would seem that this God, Creator, Love Himself, would know what we need and automatically begin to fill every available space He could with what would cause the most light to be dispersed through our lives.

How often I find myself in this position since it is a natural inclination of the flesh man to pursue what drives it to become more "happy" or feel more important in life's scenarios. But imagine what could happen if we simply laid down our preconceptions, our own imaginative solutions, and just made a place for divine love to come and find a place of rest in our home, our "temple", our persona. What if we made an addition onto our lives, say, an addition to our busy schedule, or our plans, or our own hopes, which made provision for the needs of others, as God is reflected in them. These are the things that this Shunammite woman provided which led to a fulfilled promise: first she asks her husband to build a room... A place. This was an intentional decision made by this Lady to give up some of her own space for someone else. Now, it couldn't have been too much of a sacrifice because she was adding to what she already had, and maybe the sacrifice lay more in her attitude to be willing to serve rather than in an actual loss of any kind. But this demonstrates how in the course of her life she began to understand that she could be of service in an unconventional and creative way for something, someone who brought good, otherwise light into her city and surrounding area. So she makes a decision, that was an intentional choice. She asked for the blessing....by making a place for it.

I must contend here that it is in giving that we receive. Jesus Himself, gives a parable of a man who was well off and he came upon the problem of not having enough room to store all of his bountiful crop. So he said "I'll tear down these barns and build bigger barns to house all my abundance" so he did. Once he had stored all of his crops, Jesus said that he said to his soul "soul you have many goods for many years to come, take your rest, eat drink, and be merry" But Jesus sadly says that God responded to him by saying "fool, this night your soul will be required of you! Then whose will those things be you have provided?"

Humankind has always found itself in a kind of "hunter-gatherer" stance in reference to survival. We were given an instinct for self preservation and as each successive generation has forged out their role in history we have evolved formidably to endure the survival of our race. We also strive to ensure the survival of our own personal desires. This can be viewed in every culture and in all civilizations.

But the one thing we often neglect and push aside is a principle as steady as gravity. It is, that in order to fill a vessel, it must be empty. If there is something already inside that vessel it must be poured out or removed. A prime example of this is a story we often recount as miraculous, but never stop to think of the one important factor which could have stopped the entire first miracle Jesus ever performed. It happened at the wedding at Cana of Galilee, this wedding festival that Jesus and his Mother attended was well underway when the host ran out of wine. Mary, Jesus' mother, came to Jesus for a solution knowing He was a man of supernatural miracles. So He commanded the servants to go get water pots, fill them up with water, and proceeded to change the water into wine...and apparently above average wine. But if there had been no empty vessels, just for the sake of making a point here, what would Jesus have to work with in bringing forth new wine?

Being raised in the home of a man perceived to be a "man of God" in whatever capacity he may serve, is not easy. And not only because it's impossible to live up to a standard expected of you by the people he serves, but also because he has usually imparted to you a sense of achieving the impossible. Most Pastors and Spiritual leaders feel they have a mandate from God to save the world, or at least part of it, and restore it back to God. This is in no way a bad thing, however when the man or woman imposes his will and vision on his family it can become an emotionally abrasive situation without their immediate knowledge. I have talked to so many adult children of Pastors and found this principle to be true. Whether it results in the making of another generation of servants, or a generation of embittered individuals rests solely upon the spiritual shoulders of the parent or the head of the family. It feels at times like walking a tight rope. Not only are these "called" men and women of God trying to meet the challenges of parenting, they also, very frequently become their families' only spiritual leader. The treatment of the belief that one is "called by God" and "set apart" is a necessity for one to stay fueled for a ministry of any kind, but in trying to negotiate that belief into the family structure it can evolve into a form of abusive Lordship over innocents. In specific, the children of many of those strong in their faith are not simply instructed and led into the belief systems of the parent, but they are enslaved in an undefined prison of hardships imposed on them. It is one thing to instruct our children and teach them to fear God and follow whatever set of principles we espouse, exposing them to the truth of God's word and making them accountable to a value system we deem necessary. But when our daily and personal lives don't match up, it sets the standard of hypocrisy higher than the principle of love. When a Pastor or strong individual, as a parent, enforces the rules of the home it must be applied in love. When a child knows the parent is loving them into truth for their own sake, it turns out as a beautiful example of how the Heavenly Father treats His own children. But when it is imposed in a dictatorial environment it will eventually become the thing that the child spends his life trying to escape. And the limits they will go to escape it, might risk their own lives and worse, their relationship with a loving God.

In my home as the child of a pastor, I many times got mixed signals. All roads didn't lead back to God, but by either oversight, or by taking on a disciplinary nature necessary to rear a family, it was communicated to us that all roads led to pleasing my Dad because in that home, and many other's who sat under his teaching, He was God's representative. Because he lived under such pressure dealing with other people's lives and problems and because he bore the burden of supposedly hearing from God for our church, we didn't always get him in his most loving and higher self form. He gave and gave until he had no more to give and my Mother enabled this because of her self sacrificial love for his ministry and the church. The majority of his time was spent helping others in the church community, and little time or energy was left for those at home who really depended upon him the most. In his generation this was thought of as noble and almost saintly to be so "heavenly minded that we're of no worldly good". When I was having problems negotiating how people, especially teachers, were treating me simply because I was from a "Preacher's" family, I felt like a complete failure because my situation had to call my Dad's attention away from the "things of God" to focus on me. From a tiny child I felt the burden of being an angel so my Dad wouldn't be bothered by me and disappointed by my inability to cope with life's challenges. I realize now that so much of it was self imposed, but it was my perceived reality. And as a child it loomed above the everyday activities of family interactions. I worshipped my father as most little girls do, and he could do no wrong. So when I got yelled at or punished out of his frustration of other things he couldn't control, or rebellious congregants, or as a result of his own burn out, I knew for sure I had to be the lowest and worst of human beings. Sister so-n-so was in the hospital dying, and I had to get a B- on that test? In my home we were always dealing with life and death situations so the things most families deemed as normal and necessary for a family's nurture and loving development were minimized. I know now this is not the norm for most Preacher's families, thank God, but I was raised in a time when the home had to suffer for the God anointed servant to flourish, and we accepted it as our lot in life and a privilege to be born as martyrs. God chose us from the beginning to be in this family, knowing we could handle it. God needed me to suffer for Him to accomplish His work on earth, it was my role to play, it was my box. Of course those attitudes are aberrations of the truth, and reading it now, it seems ludicrous that if a man cannot handle his own family, how can he handle anymore? It wasn't that my dad couldn't handle a family, we just never were his main priority. And that lasted throughout my entire life, I tried to shake the feeling of being second best of never being good enough to earn the affection, which for a child translates as love, of the one man I worshipped and tried to emulate. It would take me almost my entire lifetime to come to terms with the fact that I wasn't the problem, no more than the child of an alcoholic is at fault for not being lovable enough to keep their parents from the bottle. We would love to think that we are the center of our parent's world. While for some this may be the case, it may also not be the best thing for the child. The raising of children is a delicate dance between giving them a sense of self accomplishment and the proper sense of their capabilities... and boosting them to a place of supremacy above others in society. We must instill within our children the sense of who they are to God, to a power higher than themselves. My Dad did some of that for me, but sometimes I feel as though my self image and concept of God's love towards me was built upon scraps that fell from the table that my dad spread for others. The only ones who truly understand what I'm saying are other pastor's children. I see it all the time, but we must all begin our journey of self discovery to understand who we are and that we are an individual who stands apart from anyone else's belief system, religion, or perceptions of God. We are given one life, that we know of, to walk our own path of discovery and spiritual enlightenment. It becomes our duty and ours alone to find ourselves inside of God's love. It's a Godly parent who allows their child the same freedom of self realization and liberty to pursue their truth as God affords his children! Freedom of choice can't be taught, it can only be released in the lives of our children and I believe that's what we will account for somewhere, somehow. But it's comforting to know there's an "Agape" loving God, who will help us through what we bring upon ourselves, either by our own ignorance, or by our choice. Sometimes we just emulate what our parent's did because that's all we know. But in our age of available Information and the technology to acquire it, we should do our best to find out the most spiritually healthy way to "train up a child". Our world is totally different than it was when I was a child, so the way my grandchildren must be reared will be given to my children as a grace from God. He gives wisdom in all things if we go to Him and seek our answers. Especially concerning future generations.

Because everything is in a flux of change, everything...down to the tiny cells that make up our bodies. And as some age quicker than others and some seem to mature slowly, each soul has its own rhythm and speed at which it changes. We cannot be afraid of moving into a new awareness of God simply because we are afraid we might be implicated in heresy. This generation has access to far more advanced tools in the study of life, and the supernatural beyond it. We must always stay true to certain standards and moral responsibilities, but we cannot be afraid to explore. Why are we in this generation? What attributes do those born right now have that assist in bringing their contemporaries to a better understanding of God. And you and I were put here, not by accident but because there is an assignment we each have within our spiritual DNA. But in order to access that part of ourselves, not only does our concept of ourselves need to be expanded, but also our concept of who and where God is must be put to the test.

Are we the "peculiar" people God has called out or not? Last days, or not, in order to ensure the return of Christ and His goodness and righteousness, we must be willing to expand, just like this universe, our goal, of course, being to expand into His likeness. But it starts with Change.

7 CHANGE OR BUST

How can it not be obvious to us that everything within our scope of present understanding is malleable and changeable? The components that make up our very atmosphere, which sustains all life is delicately balanced and we understand now, enlightened by time and experience, that they can be changed. They can be altered to perform any number of things. The elements present to sustain us, can also be turned to destroy us. It doesn't take a rocket scientist to know that if certain elements are combined, they are combustible. But combined in the correct proportions, they are necessary for the sustaining of life. Just one example is the the element of hydrogen. With my limited knowledge of chemistry, I know that hydrogen changes depending on the environment, most of us just accept this and take it for granted, but for those of us who need a reminder, I'll cite this:

"Hydrogen is the most abundant element on the planet and is therefore one of the most important. It is a highly combustible element, which makes it very useful in areas where it's needed, such as in fuels."

"Hydrogen is the first element on the periodic table and thus has an atomic number of one. It occurs naturally in the environment and two hydrogen atoms combine with one atom of oxygen produce water. Hydrogen is commonly used to break down unsaturated vegetable oils and to obtain solid fats. It can also be burned in combustion engines."

One of the major ways that hydrogen is used in the body is in water. Water is made up of two-thirds hydrogen atoms. According to the Mayo Clinic, water is so important that it makes up over sixty percent of your body. Because of hydrogen, the cells are able to remain hydrated, toxins and waste are able to be eliminated from the body, nutrients are able to be transported to the cells that need them, your joints are lubricated, and your body's immune system is able to send defensive cells to fight off infection-causing fungus, bacterias and viruses.

Introduce that same element into another environment and this transpires..."Flammability...Hydrogen is extremely flammable. It is highly volatile and can cause explosions when it is introduced into the air or mixed with other gases. Metal catalysts can make these explosions even more violent. All flammable substances should be removed from areas where a hydrogen leak is suspected or has been confirmed. Fortunately hydrogen dissipates quickly in well-ventilated areas."

*Additional resources...: ehow.com, Cha-Cha.com

As dismissive as we can be concerning these things, it's a good thing to occasionally revisit the truths of the created universe that sustains our present life form, which is known as "human". But we rarely think of these elements from which we take life because they were assembled eons ago to do a job, accomplish a purpose and put us on our track of destiny. From wherever you think we came or from whatever we took form, there is no denying that elements change. As does everything else in this created universe. How presumptuous of us as a life form, and not the only one of importance on this tiny ball of a planet, to think that we set the rules for all time and eternity and if these rules are violated or changed then consequences, which we usually contrive, will be inevitable. In the written Word we are given the primer on what never changes...this is what we are told...

"For Jesus doesn't change—yesterday, today, tomorrow, He's always totally himself."
Hebrews 13:8 MSG

There are a few other things that I will bring out at another time that we might add to this list. But my point is, that we are never told we will never change, in fact we are being "transformed" into the image of "His dear Son" and of course there are very few stipulations put on that. The way we understand this process of transformation is to look at nature. The word "transformed" or "metamorphoo" (Gr.), in these passages, gives us the picture of the metamorphosis of the caterpillar into the butterfly. This process of changing is not instantaneous nor is it easy. The caterpillar goes through several stages before the beautiful butterfly emerges. It starts with an egg which hatches into the caterpillar, which is the larvae. The caterpillar then grows by it's constant eating and becomes an adult. The third stage is when the caterpillar forms itself into a pupa or chrysalis and again it undergoes and endures extreme change. And finally, in the fullness of time, the butterfly emerges in it's perfected state. It's not by accident that this particular word is used to describe our process of becoming God's sons. We undergo extreme, sometimes uncomfortable, changes until we emerge in our perfected state looking like our elder brother Jesus. Maybe endurance through these changes is what saves us. This bears out in scripture when it says that "he that endures to the end, the same shall be saved"! But everything, everything changes, except for God Himself, however it is noted in an Old Testament scripture that even God changed his mind about destroying mankind, whether that's a foundational truth or just added to this passage for emphasis, we only know that the writer, through inspiration, deduced that God changed the course of His actions.

We live in a universe rife with change. It is ever being manipulated by an unseen force. It is even now, expanding away from us. No one knows the final outcome of life's condition on this earth or in this universe. But, we do have a hope, if we believe in redemption and a God always reaching for us, even though the universe is expanding outward He is coming ever closer to fulfill His plan.

Now, I want to establish that good can find a way to flourish in places born out of oppression, cruelty, or just done through ignorance. Picture here a concrete sidewalk, and sticking up through a tiny crack in the concrete is a little yellow flower. That's how goodness and godliness are, in the hard times, they just push a little harder to make their presence known. All it needs is the tiniest place of receptivity.

I want to share a personal experience with you along the lines of emptying out, to make space for the new and to surrender the place to someone else in need...and in return getting something even better! Life changes and evolves and so should we, where we were and what we needed six months ago is oftentimes already different from where we are and what we need today. We are a living organism and our God-part is always striving to get back to God by being more like him. We are living in the continual process of this over and over again since we were made a vessel designed to pour and not contain.

I want to share an opportunity given to me and my family that would ultimately stretch us into a position to receive and turn our lives around. Maybe you'll identify on some level. One of the good things that flourished in my childhood home was the relationship I had with my sisters. We were forced many times into finding comic relief and to watch out for one another in our daily walk. I had two sisters one six years my senior and one ten years my senior. There had been times before I was born or right afterwards when my sisters were subjected to certain things that bred insecurities within them and not always by our parents, sometimes it was just through the circumstances that surround any church or institution of religion.

When I was born I was very celebrated because my mother had experienced such hardships in having me. Before I was conceived she had been through two miscarriages and one was ectopic and destroyed one of her ovaries. So, me being conceived, had somewhat of a miraculous quality. All the women in the church were the preacher's wife's cheerleaders and so when I was born I became a "church" baby. I've been told I was doted on for the first six months of my life, meaning, everyone wanted to hold me, and see how my mother dressed me, which was usually in all frills.

One amusing story surrounds my grandfather, who was known as "The Walking Bible" by the denomination in which he served. He had been saved as a young man and received the "baptism of the Holy Spirit" at the behest and ministry of my very beautiful grandmother. He was only able to complete a few years of grade school. In those days in the South, when you got strong enough to work the farm, being a farm hand became the priority. My family lived off the land, the crops, animals, and land were their life sustaining possessions. But my Grandaddy, with very little education had to quit school and become a plow hand or do whatever he could to help make the farm profitable. When he married my grandmother who was herself the daughter of a farmer, he wanted to learn some things. God had put him with the right woman because she had been the favored daughter by her father and was given kitchen duty with her mother. She never had to go out in the sun and work or harvest the crops. And if she did go outside he made her don a hat. She was a true "Southern Bell" and had the education to show for it. So when she married my grandfather she taught him how to read. She taught him with the best possible text book, the bible. My Granddaddy would read long into the night even by candlelight. And as he did, he would memorize the scriptures as his own. So, naturally when he was called into the ministry it worked to his advantage to know the scripture by wrote.

He became his denomination's national radio voice on a weekly broadcast and in those days they were not usually taped, but broadcast from a studio live. I was born early on a Sunday morning, my parent's third daughter, fat and healthy. I don't know how my Granddaddy got the message of my birth, but he only got the news that he had another healthy granddaughter. I don't know if my parents had named me yet or not, but I do know my birth was announce to a listening audience and I was dubbed "Deborah". My parents said that name was never even a consideration but only my sweet

Granddaddy, a power house in a short robust stature, would so confidently make such an assertion and feel good about it!! My sweet Granddad!! So at first many people thought I was "Deborah", but I had been given another name which would come to have much meaning over the course of my life. Of course my birth was regaled and all the church ladies just thought I was a doll.

My sister Becky took immediately to the role she would so often play as my surrogate mother. She would forever protect, defend, and comfort me until the day she went to be with God. But my other sister who was six at the time, didn't take to the whole experience very well. And rightfully so, she felt a little slighted because in one fell swoop her whole world changed with the birth of this little thing. One day she overheard my mother talking to another lady as ladies do, and she was remarking about how pretty I was as a newborn, round head, pink cheeks...fat rolls and all! She had no idea that my sisters were listening in. She had already made them leave to go play and when they did see me she made them wear little masks because they had been sick. Then she said something just in passing that cut my sister to the heart when she said, "well I think she is my prettiest baby"! My sister immediately ran and cried...needless to say, our relationship was not as close as the relationship I had with my older sister. But she eventually became a good big sister, watching out for me in times when I wasn't even aware. She also provided our comic relief, especially at night when we were told to go to bed after our family prayer. We would get in our beds, Joy in hers, Becky and and I in our shared bed, and she would begin to say things to make us laugh. Part of what made this all so humorous was that we knew if our Daddy heard us, he would soon be walking heavily down the hallway to dole out our dreaded punishments. On many occasions, he would just warn us about "one more time", but we just couldn't resist the urges to giggle, and belly laugh quietly. On some nights, Becky, who loved to laugh more than anyone I've ever known, would ask Joy to come out into our adjoining hallway and perform a dance. We had a song we would sing that only we knew and Joy would proceed to do an interpretive dance that would totally take our breath away with laughter. The song was called

"Ahhhh, Lemon Choni Ma" sounds crazy, and I don't even know it's origin but I can still sing it today. On one of these occasions, we heard the door to my parents room creek open and my dad's footsteps. Joy didn't have time to make it to her bed so she quickly ran and got in our bed with me on top of her, and Becky adjusted the sheet to hide her, her head under my pillow. By the time my dad got there we were in a state of hysteria hoping my dad wouldn't notice. But he did, as I was moving up and down with every gasp of air Joy would take. At first he didn't say a thing, in fact he just stood there, conversing with us...all the while knowing Joy was holding her breath and would have to appear from under the covers soon. He took his sweet time, knowing this was a much more effective punishment for our antics. Finally, having gasped for air long enough, Joy sprang up throwing me off of the bed as she took in gulps of air. We all laughed, even Daddy, who let us off the hook this time. We had many of these episodes during the time that the three of us lived at home.

As we grew and each moved out of the house in our respective order, the chemistry between each of us would change many times, but the one thing that never changed was my older sister's love and concern for me. I won't say there was never a small amount of vying for parental attention, especially from my Daddy, who was the voice of God to us, but we remained close. My older sister Becky married a man from California, a strong loving prophetic man who had been a high school football coach in Corona Del Mar in California. There wasn't a night in my life that Becky and I had not been bedmates until she got married. This was a shock for an eight year old girl!! Sam felt so bad for taking my bedmate from me that he bought me the biggest stuffed Pooh Bear he could find as a substitute sleeping partner. But I soon found that Pooh couldn't talk to me, dream with me, tell me stories, sing with me, or dry my tears.

When my sister Becky moved back to our home state of Georgia, after moving to California for a year as a newlywed, she and her husband desired to buy a farm as a homestead. My brother-in-law, Sam, being a former football coach had always wanted to raise Black Angus cattle. So they took what money they had, which was small, and invested it in acreage for a cattle farm. Upon this acreage stood an old dilapidated farmhouse. They had no money to improve it or build something better. As a young girl and teenager I spent many hours there, just being with Becky, wandering the farm, and also spending time with my nephew when he was born.

If you set your mind to think of an old farmhouse, probably built equipped with outhouse and all the other farm style "luxuries", you can picture their deteriorating house. But Becky, with her creativity and talent for cozy charm made it a home. I loved being there, but I didn't enjoy sitting on the toilet seat which drastically slanted to one side because of an uneven floor. And everything in it was small and lacking. However, it never stopped my sister and brother-in-law from graciously welcoming those with spiritual needs into their little home for a time of ministry. Once Sam was ordained as a pastor, and Becky ordained as a teacher of the Word, by every right a pastor herself, they were always available to counsel, comfort, and pray for those in need.

The home itself was not very conducive to this and neither were, by this time, three boys running under foot! But they never let that deter their passion to minister. The time came for them to rebuild another house because the state needed to buy a part of their frontage to widen the highway and they would either take the offer or have the county condemn the house they were in, but they really didn't have the resources to build. However, they knew it was a faith journey and if they moved ahead God would provide. And he did!!

The congregation stepped up volunteering their services. Businesses within the congregation donated whatever was needed, and soon a beautiful country home donned the hill just beyond them ....trees flanking both sides of a long winding driveway. The time came for my sister and her family to move into the house, but they had little to no furnishings. I don't believe it was ever a thought in my sister's mind that she would get new furniture, she was already overwhelmed by the outpouring of love that had brought them to this point.

My husband and I were in a similar place at this time, needing to expand, but under different circumstances. During our dating years and early marriage my husband was a builder carrying on the legacy of the family trade. I myself was eking out a small supplemental income working at a company that specialized in publishing and collating real estate ad books. We lived in a one bedroom flat and barely got by on a very small income, but things were moving ahead for us. We also both fulfilled roles of ministry at the church where my Dad pastored, so that left us no spare time. Wes, working in electronics had begun taping the church services. And I sang in various groups, taught Sunday school and helped in editing books that were being written from my dad's sermons. When we had been married a little over six months Wes began desiring to pursue a different profession that would bring in more money. So he ventured out and began taking classes to become an electronic technician with the intention of going to work for the transit system in our city or working for an Atlanta based airline. Having married young, it was a priority for us to fulfill our desire to establish our independence and we were determined to do so. So while my husband worked during the day and went to school at night, I was working my job, and trying hard to provide a comfortable home. However after nine months of working to fit into our new roles, I discovered that I was expecting our first child, and it was a surprise!! So much so that my husband who was already over worked not only went into a temporary state of shock, but fell rapidly into a state of depression. I think both of our parents, being aware of our situation, were concerned that we were going to began encountering problems, so my Dad, in his concern offered me a job as a part time receptionist which paid more than my current job. I was relieved to say "yes!" I stood on my feet 8 hours a day assembling books and my pregnant body would be able to sit for my new job. At the same time, my Dad offered to pay Wes for the work he was already doing at the church. Thankfully, this helped provide a more comfortable lifestyle and lessened our struggle. Eventually Wes was able to build us a small house where we would welcome our little boy. It was a very small house but it was ours!! Ownership never felt so good! But as our family grew so did our opportunity to minister and within a few years we were hosting a meeting in our small home for young families. To say our house was too small to accommodate 30 adults and their children would be an understatement! On top of that I had furniture borrowed or given to me by my gracious Mother-in-law and it was showing signs of fatigue, such as holes in the sofa and broken table legs. I did what I could to make it presentable covering the sofa with sheets and pins and using tray tables together under a table cloth. The day came when finally we had saved enough money to began making payments on a new sofa and chair. The day we went to pick out that furniture was a wonderful day!! And I was so excited to be able to offer our guests a nice seating arrangement. So we dutifully began making our payments and set the day for the furniture to be delivered. This is where God created an opportunity for a miracle, but I didn't see it coming or recognize it in the beginning. As we were preparing to "redecorate" our home out of necessity, my sister was preparing to move into hers. I will never forget the Sunday our intended plans collided to create the atmosphere for a life changing experience.

8 THE TEARS OF SACRIFICE

Before I finish this story, I want you to go back to a time, anytime in your life, when you had to give up something you loved. A time you still remember that is etched in your memory, when you had to let go of something or someone you loved. Whether you considered it a noble sacrifice or a sacrifice that was simply done out of necessity, just call it into your mind's eye. Now, although you may not appreciate having to relive it, just allow the feeling of loss you had, maybe even abandonment along with that. Or maybe you lost something upon which hinged your hope for a brighter future, or maybe rejection played a role and you reacted by relenting, but you still lost something.

It's this kind of sacrifice I speak of when I propose that sacrifice is a key to accessing spiritual abundance manifested in an earthly way. The scripture we used on my sister, Becky's headstone when she died a premature death was "except a seed fall unto the ground it remains alone, but if it falls into the ground and dies, in due time, it will produce a harvest" Jesus said that. I am under the firm belief that our Father, creator and cosmic lover catches every tear of sacrifice that spills from our eyes and puts them in a bottle, that's how the scripture depicts his care for us. And this bottle then is miraculously turned into the water of life for our very souls. And just when we need it, just when we're parched with disappointment, or illness and disease or disillusionment, he begins to pour it over us and restore to us our very lives!! This is what took place in this situation on a very important Sunday morning. The Sunday service was in progress and everyone had been singing in worship and praise in anticipation of the day, which was our custom. And then came the time for a prayer. In the middle of our songs of praise and worship one of our various pastors on the staff, who numbered in doubled digits now, would be asked to say a prayer to set the service in motion. On this particular Sunday the pastor who got up to pray was a man known for his ability to speak God's insight into people's situations. He began by saying, "I have a word for someone and I'm not sure who." What he proceeded to say would rock me. He then began to talk about my sister and her husband and how everyone who had contributed would be blessed. "But" he said "God's not finished yet, when God does a thing he does it right." And he said that God wouldn't leave this dear family with an unfurnished home, and that someone in that service had the furniture which belonged to them. Now he said it more like that than like an opportunity for someone to give. It was more along the lines that somebody had bought this furniture unknowingly, particularly for my sister's home. I stood there for a moment trying to grasp the meaning of his words, and suddenly it dawned on me, "maybe God's speaking to me?" So I said in my heart, "God if you're speaking to me, let me know." No sooner had that thought permeated my heart than I heard the words similar to, "you might have bought this furniture thinking it was for you, but it's not!" My heart sunk because immediately I thought of the long awaited furniture being delivered to my little house that week. For the next hour and a half I wrestled with my will and I reasoned within myself about how justified I would be in keeping the furniture, after all, maybe someone else in the congregation would step forward and we could both have nice new furniture, we deserved it! But the more I thought about surrendering my will to God the more detached I felt from the beautiful country blue chair and sofa with wood details that I had been picturing in my own living room. Immediately after the service I went to Wes and told him my thoughts.

One thing about a caring spouse is they usually know when

you're serious and he looked dead into my eyes and asked me if I was sure. Of course I was sure, but I didn't have joy about it yet! When we told my sister that we had just bought a sofa and chair and it would be delivered to their home within a week, my sister cried. At first they wouldn't accept it, but as I began to reassure them that I just had to do it knowing it was the right thing, they relented. I did shed a few tears, but eventually, I found a peace and let it go. Several months later, through some unseen circumstances, we were able to purchase a piece of land down the street and Wes began the arduous task of building us a more fitting home. It took him a year working primarily alone with short reprieves when friends might stop by to help. But he built us a beautiful much larger home! As he built every one of our needs would be met. And when we moved in I also, through a set of miraculous circumstances, got just about every room in my home furnished with new furniture!! God was testing, not only my ability to recognize Him, but to also be willing to give up anything for Him. It was in the basement of that home that our church, which would last for 16 years, began. It truly was a house of ministry and God so richly blessed us. He did multiply my giving by probably more than 100 fold! And the best part was when I discovered that the furniture I gave up was going into the prayer room at my sister's home! There, people would be seated when she and her husband ministered hope and healing to dozens, probably hundreds of people, myself and my husband included!

This demonstrates the principle of being emptied for the blessing, then being willing to turn around and bless someone else with it, releasing it to be used through productivity into the world for God. Then we can prepare to receive the higher deposit God will make which will far exceed the first. It's exponential and works with more than just physical possessions. It also works with kindness, forgiveness, joy, hope, help, and in many other things. Including our enlightenments, our wisdom, our love. This principle currently stands as one of the major necessities for this light force to dwell in us around us, and show through us to a greater intensity. Although we were created and constructed to house this power and be a conduit through which it is released into this realm, the Creative force, who is God, will force none of this upon us. Love "is", He is the "I Am" of the ages.

One of the first encounters we find in the scriptures of God interacting with man to reignite in him the truth of who we are is found in the book of Exodus. Moses, the man chosen to lead "God's chosen" people out of slavery was confronted with this force which manifested by fire. The story is conveyed to us in such a way as to show us that the method by which God got Moses' attention and total commitment to this cause of deliverance was by advancing His knowledge of truth in one fell swoop. God determined the only way in which to get this man's undivided attention was by splitting through the atmosphere around Moses and showing up In the form of fire. Which is so easily understood as a source of this light and passion. This is how the story goes:

"Moses was shepherding the flock of Jethro, his father–in–law, the priest of Midian. He led the flock to the west end of the wilderness and came to the mountain of God, Horeb. The angel of God appeared to him in flames of fire blazing out of the middle of a bush. He looked. The bush was blazing away but it didn't burn up. Moses said, "What's going on here? I can't believe this! Amazing! Why doesn't the bush burn up?" God saw that he had stopped to look. God called to him from out of the bush, "Moses! Moses!" He said, "Yes? I'm right here!" God said, "Don't come any closer. Remove your sandals from your feet. You're standing on holy ground." Then he said, "I am the God of your father: The God of Abraham, the God of Isaac, the God of Jacob." Moses hid his face, afraid to look at God. God said, "I've taken a good, long look at the affliction of my people in Egypt. I've heard their cries for deliverance from their slave masters; I know all about their pain. And now I have come down to help them, pry them loose from the grip of Egypt, get them out of that country and bring them to a good land with wide–open spaces, a land lush with milk and honey, the land of the Canaanite, the Hittite, the Amorite, the Perizzite, the Hivite, and the Jebusite."The Israelite cry for help has come to me, and I've seen for myself how cruelly they're being treated by the Egyptians. It's time for you to go back: I'm sending you to Pharaoh to bring my

people, the People of Israel, out of Egypt." Moses answered God, "But why me? What makes you think that I could ever go to Pharaoh and lead the children of Israel out of Egypt?" "I'll be with you, " God said. "And this will be the proof that I am the one who sent you: When you have brought my people out of Egypt, you will worship God right here at this very mountain." Then Moses said to God, "Suppose I go to the People of Israel and I tell them, 'The God of your fathers sent me to you'; and they ask me, 'What is his name?' What do I tell them?" God said to Moses, "I–AM–WHO–I–AM. Tell the People of Israel, 'I–AM sent me to you.' "
Exodus 3:1-14 MSG

This fire, or light was all consuming but never consumed any matter around it...in other words it was generated through love, so this fire was revealing God's true essence and nature. The phenomenon was commanding Moses' attention and revealing to him the task at hand, which would demand a high price from this man and necessitate total trust and reliance upon the creative power available to him. He was once the son of a Pharaoh, regal and proud, but now, he is standing in the desert places being asked to empty himself of all of his own preconceived ideas of himself and become the son and leader God needs. And once his attention is secured God begins revealing to Moses who He is with this "I Am" concept.

In recent years and months the "I Am" principle has captivated seekers of truth. Since the foundation of all things is found in Him and seen and experienced through Him (whether He's acknowledged or not), we have to believe that because He is all encompassing, He is everywhere always. And He is the Grand sum of all our parts. And we can direct more of His ability through us by embracing the understanding that because He is the "I Am" we are the collective through which He displays Himself. However there must be a willing cooperative for Him to work with and through. us. The "God" place, which dwells in each of us by design, has to be recognized and initiated in our lives, otherwise the ever abiding human nature to limit ourselves to a one dimensional existence will prevail.

Moses, emptied himself of regal royalty and chose instead supernatural power!! He emptied himself to get what he needed from the "I AM" so he could receive his divine assignment.

9 THE DECISION TO EXPAND AND BUILD

Have you ever thought about how the on going survival of our planet is completely dependent on how different species fulfill their role in nature? An amazing example of this is the sea turtle. At one point in our lives we owned beach real estate. God blessed us to be able to purchase several condos in Florida on the Gulf of Mexico. When we first begin to visit and stay there I noticed stakes placed in the sand in an orderly fashion as if to lay down boundaries. Tied between the stakes was orange tape blowing in the breeze. One day I walked down to check out this situation and noticed somewhat of a little mound of sand in the middle of it. The stakes were there to protect a sea turtle nest. I soon came to realize that the beach patrol took the protection of this endangered species serious. We would often go down by the water and erect a tent for our family to enjoy during the hot hours of the day. When the day was over and we began to leave, we would often leave the tent frame in place so that it would be there for us the next day. We had only done that a few times when one morning upon arriving at the tent there was a tag tied to the tent frame. It was a warning that leaving anything on the beach overnight would result in a hefty fine, and why? Because when the sea turtles hatched there could be no obstructions in their way of making it down to the water. Each of these "clutches" of eggs contains from 90-180 hatchlings but the sad truth is that only five out of the 200 tiny turtles survive. If you've ever witnessed the moment when the turtles begin to hatch it is phenomenal to watch, these little creatures come bursting out of the sand one right after another fighting their way out and immediately making a mad dash for the sea. Sadly, on stand by, are several predators who also like to witness the hatchlings so they can have a meal. The reason the sea turtles lay so many eggs is so that some have a better chance of survival. But what about the ones who give up their lives? Were they not important? I've often wondered why these little guys can't just hatch in a safe place away from the predator's clutches! But it's meant for a certain amount of these little guys to be eaten so others can live. It's a sacrifice to be conceived, formed, and birthed just to be somebody's meal!! But when a life is created for sacrifice that giving up of its life is precious to God! And even though they will most likely meet their doom, they fight for their little lives. There are so many examples on this earth of the necessity for sacrifice in order to gain life or food or to simply survive.

Few of us can truly understand sacrificing our lives for the sake of the continuation of someone else's life. The closest human beings to experience this would most likely be those who choose a life in the military, or emergency responders, such as law enforcement or even a fire fighter. Those who risk their own well being for others demonstrate this principle. John the Baptist, the cousin of Jesus was very aware that for Jesus and His life and ministry to prosper, that John himself would have to decrease and his pride and ego be sacrificed. Sometimes that is the hardest sacrifice of all, our own notoriety or reputation. Of course Jesus Christ Himself did this exact thing, He became of no reputation so that He could become the light of the world. And in this regard the Shunammite woman is a general reflection of His divine sacrifice.

The Shunammite woman we read about truly displays for us a wealth of crucial information about how to sacrifice in order to apprehend and continue with all we'll ever need. "I'm certain," said the woman to her husband, "that this man who stops by with us all the time is a holy man of God. Why don't we add on a small room upstairs and furnish it with a bed and desk, chair and lamp, so that when he comes by he can stay with us?"

She knew that if she built it, he would come. No matter how passionate we may or may not be about about apprehending God's provisions and blessings in our lives, the same is true across the board, we must make room for them. It is the belief in this truth, that if we open ourselves and start making a new place, new things will come, new things will begin to manifest, things which ultimately take us to our destiny.

God, His light, His provision, His blessing, His ministry, His love is always on the move in this world. God's spirit is ever seeking places to fill, but here's the thing, if we leave a void empty, without preparation for what we desire along the lines of goodness, darkness will settle in. Darkness automatically fills up any empty space of desire you leave unattended in your life. Be it an emotional lack for acceptance, a desire to be noticed, even a desire for ministering and helping others, which without proper direction and oversight can lead to counterfeit and ofttimes harmful substitutes. Voids don't stay empty long and because we were created to house something to be a container of light and love, we will contain something. There can be no neutral territory. There are times at dusk or dawn when light comes to penetrate darkness or darkness comes to overtake light when we can see the conversion of this process taking place. These are both beautiful and serene times, spewing colors out across the sky in vivid arrays of shades. But the one thing they share is that there is always that time, either before the Sun sets or rises, that without any artificial assistance it's hard to see. We must always keep in mind that our primary job is to shed the light of love into the atmosphere. The displays that come into our lives can be beautiful when the sun is rising and bringing a new day, but they can be just as beautiful when the sun is giving way to darkness. We can't be fooled into thinking that simply because it appears a certain way to us, that it is leading in the right direction. Those beautiful displays can fool us!

This story of the woman beautifully illustrates how life can lead us somewhere or into an unforeseen situation even when we are just doing what we would normally do. This lady in the story is referred to as a "leading lady" in her community so we can only surmise that she was accustomed to having a notable social standing. Therefore it is reasonable to believe that she would be one who would entertain the important people who came to town. Although a "prophet" was not necessarily hailed with celebrity status as he would be today, she recognized the possibilities in opening a place for him.

This story is full of contradictions and misrepresentations, yet it brings a truth of what this life, life on this planet in a hostile environment for us can be. We are made as agents to be filled with light and love, but we can expect to run into hardships in order to be emptied time and time again, to make place for more of this love we are destined to display. The prophet, considered to be God's very voice and representative on planet earth for this time in this culture's history frequently travels through this city, Shunem, for whatever reason. He is being sent on a mission and he runs into this important lady who obviously holds some ability to be persuasive, as she is able to convince this man of God to stop by her place for dinner. It seems from the story that we are given, that she has no ulterior motive other than simply to provide a place for the empowerment of "good" in her life, and in so doing she made a "room" or place for a miracle.

A "miracle" can be defined as the place where the supernatural meets the natural... with the supernatural holding so much more sway over the recipient, that the natural must succumb! And it's illustrated perfectly for us in this story. She said to her husband "lets fix a small room for him", a "small" room. What would have been possible if she had made a larger place? Well she didn't but what she did do is equip this place with useful commodities that would serve to be very valuable. This is what I see in examining how she decided to furnish this room given over to house God's voice in the land.

10 THE BED

This noble lady makes room for a miracle by providing a place for heaven or the supernatural unseen realm, and the natural realm to collide. When this happens, the greater force of life will always prevail. making the impossible, possible. But we must pay close attention to the example she sets forth by properly furnishing her "God" place. First she provides a bed. A bed in its most basic function is a place upon which most of us rest. We think of the bed in terms of providing a cradle of comfort in which to receive our rest and sustenance and vigor for life. Without which, we ultimately become weak and finally totally unproductive altogether. It is more than just a place, the bed represents a place of vulnerability because when we sleep we must shut down our defenses, our thoughts and we have a systematic shut down of all of our functions so that we can regenerate. But while we're in our sleep state, we are also physically vulnerable. We must entrust our care to others. But one can also surmise that the "bed" can be symbolic of a place to express love, share secrets, become intimate and spark new life!

Lovers share intimacies that are only known to the two of them. There are words and phrases that form out of romantic bonds that we identify with certain relationships. At least in my experience and through observation it is clear that even a glance from someone you've been intimate with, holds a significant amount of information... the eyes being the "windows to the soul", but you also usually have a song you share that defines a special moment in your relationship. You have little words or signals most can't pick up on that have meaning to only the two of you, and no matter how many others have experienced "you" in this capacity, it's never the same chemistry with any two people. So only the two of you know the feelings and moments shared! God is the same with each of us! Extraordinarily, He can have moments and words and songs and feelings and whispers with you that no one else would understand. And every relationship you have is different, it feels a certain way. But this one thing is true, a relationship must be grown, it must be nurtured into maturity. And it takes the investment of ourselves and our most precious commodity, time. There must be trust to have complete and total vulnerability and productive intimacy. We have so cheapened the act of intimacy between sexual partners in this culture by sharing our "bed" and exchanging intimacies with strangers that we don't intend to form a relationship with. And we waste time and energy in flirtations that lead to encounters for the express purpose of fulfilling our flesh. Once the flesh gets what it wants we discard that person. We have a toss away substitution for real love that gives sexual satisfaction a higher billing than Love. But once you've known the intimacy that comes in a trusted relationship, you realize there is no substitute. I personally don't know how people can be intimate with others they don't know or know little about. I understand instantaneous attraction but that should lead to more time to foster trust and not just to a sexual liaison. There must be love present or our bed becomes like a "sounding brass and a tinkling cymbal" which was the Apostle Paul's description of any kind of social action not done in love. The intention and motivation of a heart is what makes it love or lust and love takes time. And we make a place for that significant other by thinking of them, reaching out to them and spending time with them. When you truly love someone you cherish the time you spend together and you do whatever it takes to enjoy more time interacting with them. It's far from being a chore, you wake up looking forward to hearing their voice, looking into their eyes, and feeling their touch. You wake up with this desire, carry it through out the day, and probably close your eyes thinking of future encounters!

This is the kind of intensity with which we should pursue and desire our divine lover! No one would argue that our greatest commodity is time. So it would stand to reason that when one is willing to give up their time energy and focus to the supernatural interactions of God's spirit, there is an exchange of the divine. The only way we will ever truly know God's heart is when we snuggle up next to Him in intimacy willing to give Him our vessel, willing to let Him fill up our very souls with His desires. The revolutionary ideas that God desires to bestow upon those He loves will only be apprehended by a complete emptying and cleaning out, and then a rebuilding of cradles to nurture the divine. Then He can trust us to hold His whispers of love until we are ready to release it in a new way. And this way will bring all humanity to liberation from darkness, evil, and pain.

When observing the actions of Christ, we see that He postured Himself in a way that appeared to challenge the status quo of His day. Although He instructed His followers to abide by the civil laws, when it came to moral mandates and the present and former Jewish laws He clearly shone a revealing light on the prevailing hypocrisy. His entire quest was to liberate men from their own devises by which they had been bound, well meaning devises in some cases, nonetheless, laws which by nature gave men authority in areas of the societal life which were designed to take away the personal freedoms of humanity that God gifted us with. His attitude far transcended the attitudes of the day where religion resided. He came in, if you will, and turned the soil of man's present condition over and over, as if tilling the ground until the weeds were exposed, weeds that were choking out the true beauty of God's fruits of love. Although as a basic human race we have come so far in the 2,000 plus years since Jesus, we still find ourselves in a moral dilemma of not understanding that morals cannot be dictated as they must come from an inner source. And that source is what must become more clear and discernible in this present age. As darkness continues to spread through out hearts and minds it is the task of the "enlightened", those who consider themselves to be lined up with Godly intentions for planet earth, to take on a new challenge of becoming more translucent, transparent, and exposed as those who know the source of humanity. And whatever people call "Him", I don't say "it" because I believe this force to be a very personal and intimate Creator who is the origin of any type of love...we know Him as God, the force of this entire cosmic condition.

And this is where the "bed" we speak of in this story about the woman who made provision for a visitation takes shape. If we intend on becoming a pure light to expose evil, cruelty, and oppression of any kind, we must know the one true source of life intimately. The way in which two people not only merge to become one but also to procreate and renew life is represented by this "bed", the place in which we become totally vulnerable and exposed as a lover. We must give our hearts, emotions, and passions to the one who actually created those very elements of life, as a lover, one truly in love, not just in lust, gives themselves over completely to the one who has captivated their thoughts. We must then learn how to hold Him inside after we have spent time communing with Him, either through prayer, mediation, or ingesting His nature by experiencing this earth and all it offers. In our churches as we participate in the partaking of what is liturgically called the "Eucharist" we celebrate this concept. Rehearsing and doing as Jesus said "in remembrance of Me", which is the eating of the "Lord's supper" and is another way in which we symbolically, or some believe, literally through "transubstantiation", ingest His divinity into our own being. We can find the kind of love I'm describing in the book of the Song of Solomon...

"All night long on my bed I looked for the one my heart loves; I looked for him but did not find him. I will get up now and go about the city, through its streets and squares; I will search for the one my heart loves. So I looked for him but did not find him. The watchmen found me as they made their rounds in the city."Have you seen the one my heart loves?" Scarcely had I passed them when I found the one my heart loves. I held him and would not let him go till I had brought him to my mother's house, to the room of the one who conceived me. Daughters of Jerusalem, I charge you by the gazelles and by the does of the field: Do not arouse or awaken love until it so desires."

Song of Solomon 3:1-5 NIV

"Place me like a seal over your heart, like a seal on your arm; for love is as strong as death, its jealousy unyielding as the grave. It burns like blazing fire, like a mighty flame. Many waters cannot quench love; rivers cannot sweep it away. If one were to give all the wealth of one's house for love, it would be utterly scorned."
Song of Solomon 8:6-7 NIV

Now turn this around, because love is reciprocal and we see that part of what we must do in order to welcome the miraculous into our own being is to become a trustworthy safe haven. It is said that one cannot truly betray or hurt you if you have no investment in them.

I will pause here to admit that this betrayal, or what I perceived as such, has been the biggest enemy in my own life and at times, has stunted my ability to fulfill my responsibilities towards God in pure ministry. And I can attest to the fact that the enemy can use this to kill us physically, destroy us emotionally, and steal our confidence, all giving rise to counterproductive forces in our lives that can literally defeat us. I speak now not just of physical vulnerability, but of emotional and spiritual vulnerability. I feel this is one reason we are warned not to be "unequally yoked" and to not have "fellowship" with the "world" and the children of darkness. These warnings are taken out of context to justify a legalism that kills. We must become open and vulnerable to a certain point to those who need love and don't yet know a relationship with their creator or we are ineffective at being like Christ or discipling and helping others. Jesus notably spent time where the "sinners" hung out, He made it a point to share at the table with them and be seen with them publicly. There have been times in my life when I was advised by people I trusted in eldership roles to break off communications with my own flesh and blood to save myself. And though I know they meant well, withdrawing myself from them only caused more pain and betrayal. Betrayal begets betrayal, and deceit spawns more deceit. It's exponential and the truth of it cannot be denied. Jesus encouraged us to be at peace with all men, and to be "peacemakers". And although there are times when it is obviously better to withdraw ourselves, our first responsibility is to do everything within our power to pursue peace. If then, it's not received, God will help us through. To be a trust worthy and peaceful being is to be a vessel of light. Let's be honest, you don't really fight fire with fire, you fight it with water. And you don't disperse darkness by removing the light, or hiding it from sight...but by turning the light up to a brighter setting. To put this in more basic terms when negative things escape our lips, they belie our true intentions, as we speak a judgmental word about someone, it sets negative forces in motion by releasing them into the atmosphere and they will take root somewhere. Most likely that place will be the most vulnerable heart or mind receiving the words! Then it just continues to grow, we are "giving place" to the darkness and multiplying evil. Conversely, if we speak loving words, they too are released and begin to produce good fruit in the hearer.

11 WHAT A BEAUTIFUL BED

If there's one thing that my husband knows it's that I can't get enough decorative pillows! Small, large, rectangle, square, round, long...I don't care as long as they're beautiful and comfortable for the most part. But I have been known to sacrifice comfort for beauty in my pillow choices, especially on my bed. Pillows make me feel warm and cozy and give me a sense of luxury that I like. I believe and practice that the right pillow can pull a room together and make it Pop!! And I love a beautiful bed! And it's not about the frame for me, I can take a mattress on the floor and make it a masterpiece, given the right sheets, comforter, blankets, shams and pillows. A bedroom should always be inviting, your favorite place to relax and take refuge. My husband, however likes to rid my bed of all its pillows, except the one he sleeps with, the moment he hits the bed. So in deference to him, I try to limit my obsession, I do want him to feel just as comfortable in our bedroom as I do. So I try to provide an inviting environment, one that is just as good for him as for me. I sort of look at my bed as a cocoon, I go in tired at night and hope by in the morning I am new. The bed is a place of rest, restoration, healing and nurture for our earthly temple. The bed I speak of now however, is the bed of the physical death of this body so that we might awake into a glorious spiritually mature being.

Go with me on the path of my own discovery so we can understand this better. I spent all of my life with an unhealthy fear of my Daddy. Though I was raised correctly to "honor your father and mother", and respect those over you in the Lord, my personality was designed to take that to the nth degree and live it in fear of my life. Somehow, I was given the signals as a child that disobedience led to death. I know it was for my own good to be trained up or have a healthy fear and respect not only of my parents and superiors, but of things I didn't understand. However, the tenacity and will power to prove myself worthy of love helped me make it through my childhood years. I did have the help of a God given protector and teacher in my sister. But, as time went by and I grew into adulthood I found myself conforming to something I wasn't sure I could even stay in stride with or believed in. My love and relationship with God was always strong, but to my detriment many times, I was not allowed the freedom to develop my own understanding of God apart from a particular kind of religious system, simply because I was born into it. At the beginning of my life our family's only desire was to please God and help people. My dad had an undeniable gift to preach and pastor because of a deep love he had for people. And there were other family members who had the gifts and callings to add to his without whose help he could not have built a church. I am only recounting my life as I saw it and lived it. Much of it is through the eyes of a child, but some is not.

In the beginning of his ministry, our church was small, family oriented and very community friendly. My Dad, uncle and others in my family brushed shoulders with MLK, Corretta, and Daddy King in fighting for justice for all of God's children. When I became a teen, we moved locations out to a suburban setting and my dad's charisma, along with great truth, and the Spirit of God brought families flooding in every service. Several movements, including a large youth ministry, nationally known, helped fuel the ministry with zeal and energy. Many came to know God, good sound teaching from the Word and healing of relationships, bodies, and lives. It was a wonderful time for everyone involved. The turn I take here, is that I knew the leader of this church not only as the great preacher, leader, author, activist, and pastor that he was, I also knew him as "Daddy". Every little girl wants to think of their dad as being invincible and capable of anything. And I was one of them. I thought anything he did had to be approved by God, and it was undergirded by a healthy dose of a congregation and leadership, along with other religious world leaders giving this credibility. My dad was brilliant and he also knew people. At one point, things began to happen around him in his relationships that previously would have raised no alarm in me because I trusted him and a child only knows what they've been conditioned to believe. As a teenager I was taught that I had to share my Daddy with others, girls like myself some of them my friends, some not, because he had to be a Spiritual Father to all. And even though in my gut I didn't like this or understand it completely, I just resisted my own inner urges to be jealous or envious. After all, I had my own challenges and though I was somewhat handicapped in social situations because of my sheltered life, I did exude an inner confidence, knowing who I was and whose I was. Most of these years were spent in a virtually hidden world of my own thoughts and questions, and though others could ask counsel of my dad on any issue, I didn't feel that freedom based on certain things that happened in my childhood. Needless to say, I lived a tortured life thinking I was crazy because I couldn't negotiate the truth I had been taught with some of the things I was sensing and feeling. But, my sisters, a caring mother along with a few friends at school, and a small but healthy youth group at the church helped me to stay afloat and make it through.

I dated a few boys, most much older than myself because I needed a male shoulder to lean on and eventually I met the boy who would become my husband. And meaning no disrespect to the man I married who has more than not been a salvation for me, I jumped at the chance to get married early and move on with the next chapter of my life. I so enjoyed my own home, being a wife and then a mother, priding myself in the loyalty and devotion we were laying down as a path for our children to follow. However, the next chapter led us back into the opportunity to minister and become involved in the ministry my family had begun years earlier. By this time it was thriving and coupled with my deep devotion to God, I couldn't say no to the call to help others. My husband and I both gave up any alternative career paths and went to work for my Dad. Several years later my own ministry had grown and I had become an ordained pastor, and mother with my own responsibilities to the congregation. And though questionable things had happened to me at the hands of others, I was insightful enough to realize that wherever there are people, there is flesh. We all need God's mercy. But I lived what I thought to be an exemplary life. Especially having been privy to some of the issues those in authority were Involved in. But the trust I maintained in my dad's ability to lead for God and protect me as his fleshly daughter was maintained at a probably unhealthy level.

I made my own mistakes, but none were a violation of the marital covenant I shared with my own husband. I'm in no way casting blame or trying to expose past issues that have been put to rest, because many others besides myself were devastated. But I began to sense something was just not right in my own marriage. I was 31, and under extreme pressure, but we both were so busy with the "work of The Lord" that we didn't devote a lot of time to what had been an otherwise peaceful and good marriage. Right after my fifteenth year wedding anniversary, a confession was made to me that shattered my world. It was betrayal at immeasurable proportions that affected my immediate household, my marriage, my children. The worst of it was that this "betrayal" had been twelve years before and my own Daddy was at the center. There was no denying it for even him. We handled it the best we knew how without it affecting anyone else, but because of the nature of the situation, I could no longer remain with the people I loved so much, or with those I had come to love as a pastor. I was near to death...I actually, regrettably, prayed to die and would have taken any avenue necessary to do so. My sister had to sit by my bed and force me to eat, and pray for my life. Looking back, I truly don't know how it could have been handled any differently. The worst part is we could tell no one by agreement of eldership because it only involved our family and I knew how many could suffer if details were revealed.

So we took the fall in the eyes of the church and family for our own preservation. But it took its toll on me and my children and has left a scar as a constant reminder of God's grace in our weakness. This would just be the beginning of a line of unexpected betrayals and hurts. I was thankfully able to forgive all offenses concerning my Dad. God didn't restore me back to the same relationship with my Dad, but to a higher revelation of my Daddy, the "man". My eyes were opened to understand how easily flesh weaknesses coupled with supernatural forces of darkness can take even the strongest man or woman on a journey of devastation. And pride in our own accomplishments or reputation, what we might define as "ego", is the biggest deterrent to a pure understanding of Love, and of God. I was with him when he died, alone, with just my daughter Penielle present. The sadness of that moment will not escape my soul for I realized it then and even more so now that it could have been much more glorious. I cast blame nowhere, but I couldn't help asking why me? Why the one who had to forgive without what most would consider an adequate apology? Why was I the one chosen to hold him, quote scripture over him pray the prayer of faith and shed tears of blood onto his face? Where were the thousands of spiritual "sons" he had groomed and poured so much of himself into.

Some visited him while he was on his deathbed, some who had been separated from him by offense. Others were never heard from. And I found out at that point that the way a man handles people in their "valley of the shadow" truly speaks to the character of that man, not the character of the dying. Thankfully some did make their way to see him or reconcile with him. I do thank my God upon every remembrance of them. And he passed, saying a few last things to me. One being that he wished he could have loved me more and that I had been the brightest star in his sky. Something every little girl wants to hear. He also commented that even the thief on the cross next to Jesus was promised "paradise".

I went on to attend to my ailing mother in my home for two years, giving up a blessed congregation that I loved with all my heart, because of all the stress and agony I allowed myself to suffer. I did my best to love and reassure her in the midst of her total life change and the feeling of being abandoned by some who promised her they would always be there for her. But sometimes my best wasn't good enough, and I understand that. And a once vivacious grandmother who could only give what little she had, one being support to her husband and those he served, was now wilting away hourly. She felt love had departed from her doors, but it had not, and we spent many blessed hours praying and conversing about the goodness of God. If anyone knew forgiveness and unconditional acceptance, it was my Mother.

One would think after such an experience in my life that trust would be hard to come by. But God has so removed my hurt as far as the east is from the west that sometimes I slip and allow myself to become hurt again. I have come to a divine conclusion that only God is trustworthy. It's the God in another human being that we trust. But there is always a chance and a risk taken when you invest in another.

We must be so careful who we become vulnerable with and though we recognize this, betrayal and devastation can come from unexpected places. What I speak of transcends the generalities of what we would call a physical place of safety. We must be trustworthy enough to protect things that are sacred. one of which is "life". Life is a valuable commodity and to be respected. Although we can acknowledge this in a moral and even spiritual sense, we must be able to practice it where the rubber meets the road. In other words, we cannot provide a place of comfort for the Divine in our lives, if we do not respect our own bodies, which were conceived as a place to house an essence, or spirit. God will come and reside and stay in a vessel that welcomes Him so profoundly that He is provided there with a place to rest His head. If we desire our God's total attention we must be willing to pay the price to keep ourselves devoid of anything that might interfere with God's nature.

In the first book of Corinthians, the Apostle tells us this:

"You know the old saying, "First you eat to live, and then you

live to eat"? Well, it may be true that the body is only a temporary thing, but that's no excuse for stuffing your body with food, or indulging it with sex. Since the Master honors you with a body, honor him with your body! God honored the Master's body by raising it from the grave. He'll treat yours with the same resurrection power. Until that time, remember that your bodies are created with the same dignity as the Master's body. You wouldn't take the Master's body off to a whorehouse, would you? I should hope not.There's more to sex than mere skin on skin. Sex is as much spiritual mystery as physical fact. As written in Scripture, "The two become one." Since we want to become spiritually one with the Master, we must not pursue the kind of sex that avoids commitment and intimacy, leaving us more lonely than ever—the kind of sex that can never "become one." There is a sense in which sexual sins are different from all others. In sexual sin we violate the sacredness of our own bodies, these bodies that were made for God–given and God–modeled love, for "becoming one" with another. Or didn't you realize that your body is a sacred place, the place of the Holy Spirit? Don't you see that you can't live however you please, squandering what God paid such a high price for? The physical part of you is not some piece of property belonging to the spiritual part of you. God owns the whole works. So let people see God in and through your body."
1 Cor 6:13-20 MSG

If you read these passages and those surrounding them, you will see how the early Christians were being taught how to respect their own bodies as "vessels" being used for a Divine purpose. Yes, God absolutely made us to enjoy living in this realm. He makes that adequately clear in many of the things said by Jesus and also in writings of the Old Testament. Many of the laws laid down by God through Moses actually are more pertinent to health and hygiene as they are to sacrifice and obedience. We are called upon to be vessels of "honor" and this necessitates a conscious effort on our part to navigate through life with a compass directing us towards improving ourselves continually, to be the very best we can be. In days gone by, many people affiliated with Christianity would use some of Jesus' other teachings about His eminent return as an excuse not to bear this out. They would talk excessively about moral sins, some of which involved violating the health of the body, but when it came to personal disciplines, such as diet and exercise, they seemed to find a way around this by conceding to the attitude of "why try, we won't be here long anyway". It wasn't just in the taking care of their bodies in which they were lax, but the justifications used by these people were flimsy and not representative at all of the way Christ Himself would have wanted us to live.

When we desecrate our bodies, it's our way of saying to God and the universe, "It's my life, my body, and mine alone to do with as I choose". I won't go into details or comparisons, but I feel we need to view ourselves as God does, as love does. As the object of a lover's desire instead of just a body of flesh surviving in a preciously chosen environment, and not necessarily one of our choosing, but one in many cases which seems to impose dangers and hostilities that mere flesh can't endure. We won't be able to think of ourselves any longer as mere mortals once we grasp the importance of our mission as love's emissaries here in this element. Once this people who are coming into their own or are in the "becoming" process truly grasp who they are, they will no longer keep their bodies fit just to live longer, they will also and more importantly do it to be fit for the purpose of being an example of God's grace and mercy. This means even in our exercising of the body it will take on a new nature, almost as if a military candidate desires to undergo boot camp and basic training to get their body prepared and in shape. They will begin desiring to be better equipped to represent this love and light to a darkening world. The caution here is that some take this to extremes making the discipline of the body through various forms of exercising, the end goal, not realizing that they don't do this unto themselves.

God calls us to be His followers, agents of love and change, and full of the light of His Grace. And sacrifice and physical torture are not deemed a part of this, no matter how it's done. We can so violate our body by running too much or breaking down muscles to rebuild them so much that it compares to smoking a pack of cigarettes a day. There are many ways in which we violate our own fleshly containers and as a consequence we are not at our best when we are needed to help someone else reconcile over to a loving God. And only God can give you the conscience you need to monitor your own health and well being. As God's seed on this earth we don't need to be abdicating our own physical care over to a system now overrun with greed and ungodly ways of treating people in need. I'm not saying don't afford yourself medical care, or insurance for it, just don't totally rely on anyone else to dictate how to care for yourself in this present world overrun by pharmaceuticals and men and women who may or may not have a "god complex" to think they can provide you with all of the answers. I believe that being a physician or working in healthcare is as much a God calling as anything else, but if love is not applied, sometimes, we are just entrusting ourselves into the hands of those who can cause more harm than good.

There's nothing more valuable to our health than a decent caring physician. But, we must never forget that our creator is the "Great Physician" and He has also placed on this earth the things required in order for us to perform to our optimum and to do our jobs with health and efficiency. It's time we stand up as children of light and help overcome oppressive medical systems however we can, even if its just in our own situation. And personally, I feel we must go to the one who has the true manual of operation concerning our temporary housing. We must make the medical system work for us and not vice versa...and only entrust our care as God's Spirit leads us. These things come only by conversations with God and through seeking and praying for wisdom. Only then can we evolve and become that generation who can truly show Christ through our spirit, soul, and body.

12 BEING BEDDED

There are other dimensions involved in providing this "bed" for God that need to be pondered. As we rest with God He then can restore and renew us. He restores our souls and renews our minds. The Psalmist said that He would use nature to restore our souls, did he not? In Psalm 23 it is stated this way, in TMB

"God, my shepherd!
I don't need a thing.
You have bedded me down in lush meadows,
you find me quiet pools to drink from.
True to your word,
you let me catch my breath
and send me in the right direction.
Even when the way goes through
Death Valley,
I'm not afraid
when you walk at my side.
Your trusty shepherd's crook
makes me feel secure.
You serve me a six–course dinner
right in front of my enemies.
You revive my drooping head;

my cup brims with blessing.
Your beauty and love chase after me
every day of my life.
I'm back home in the house of God
for the rest of my life."

I love this version of the 23rd Psalm. It says that He "makes us to lie down" or "beds" us down in green pastures and leads us beside quiet or still waters. And in so doing He restores, or gives back, or re-breathes His breath back into our souls, our lives. This is one of my favorite parts because it is exactly how I have felt from the time I was a child. The bible says "nature itself teaches us" but the psalmist is conveying here a truth that we as comfort creatures have a hard time grasping.

Driven to Lie Down

When we think of being "bedded" or forced to bed, rest isn't always what comes first to mind. The Psalmist said "He" God who is also love, "makes" us to lie down. In my studies I find it interesting that Greek, Hebrew, and any off shoot of the biblical languages always relays and communicates concepts rather than simple words. That's why it can be so difficult to thoroughly understand what is being conveyed through simple English. The concept being depicted in the phrase, he "maketh", or "makes" me to lie down, is a concept of a circular corral. Similar to the method used by herders or farmers to guide animals into certain areas. Just picture, if you will, sheep being herded by the dogs into their pins, the pin itself my have twists and turns, but ultimately it leads the sheep to their place of safety. A place where they can be observed and better protected by the shepherd. When sheep are out to pasture, they usually have to be forced to get in their pin. Therefore it is often necessary to use something they are naturally afraid of to keep them on track. I just had a Eureka moment when this was brought to my mind. Why do sheep herders use dogs to move the sheep? Well, dogs are the descendants of the natural predator and major threat to the sheep, the wolf. How awesome is this that something the sheep thinks is intended for their harm, is used by their shepherd to bring them to safety? Think about times in your life when you have been going through something and it just seems as if the circumstances of your life are going to drive you crazy! We call them "Job" seasons around my house. In reference to Job the man who God allowed to be tested for his faithfulness. Well. If God is in charge of your life, if He is your Shepherd, He is directing your path, and if on that journey you encounter hardships or loss and grief, then your Good Shepherd must know what it takes to "make" you to lie down. To lead you to conform to His will, thus keeping you safe. Why would a Good Shepherd lead us to danger? He wouldn't, most of the time those things that appear to us to be an attack of enemy forces, or the cruel fate of disobedience are God simply leading us to where we need to go. If we could grasp this, those things that caused stress in our lives would disappear for us and transform into messengers of truth. What appears to be the wolf hunting and seeking, may just be the the Shepherd's emissaries forcing you to your destiny!! So in times of hardship we need to just go with the flow.

I realize this is easier said than done, but I have learned that it's in the hard places in my life where ministry and truth have been born. It would take too long to write of all the things I've experienced, but one that came to mind recently is nothing short of a miracle. Months ago, my daughter-in-law found out she was expecting. What a joy and sweet surprise! And if that wasn't enough, my daughter also became expectant. Two grandkids at once is like heaven for this grandmother! It's been exciting preparing for these two new souls, both observing and participating. Not long ago, I was at my son's home and I was led back to their bedroom to see the new bassinet which will be by their bed. As I looked at the sweet soft sheets and the little blanket, my mind immediately went to a sheet I have hidden away in my closet. But this sheet is not soft or pretty, instead it is dirty and bloody. It's sealed away with pictures of a vehicle, a jeep to be exact, that is demolished and torn up, the morbid picture of an accident that stopped time and drove me to utter dependency on God. My husband and I always felt as if we had raised our children in the fear and admonition of the Lord. We had dedicated them to God and His service as newborns and they had been in training all of their lives to bring light into darkness and minister to those in need. Our son was a specimen of spiritual zeal and charisma. He had led a youth ministry, beginning at fifteen years of age, that got noticed by "Frontline" a news television journal that aired on NPR weekly. He had been an exemplary child, always surprising us with the capabilities he possessed beyond his years. He was in seminary and married and was assisting me in the pastoral responsibilities of the church we had birthed. Due to some family stresses with my parents, such as a cancer diagnosis and some legal issues they were facing in their ministry, I felt I could not continue to put my whole heart and mind into the church. It was our intention to gradually hand the major working of our church over to hands that we felt were trustworthy. Our son had been given many encouragements and prophecies by many men and women who were considered spiritual leaders of the day concerning his future. There was no end to what he could do for God and it was a joy to behold as a mother. There came a time in my heart, a mother's intuition I guess, when I knew that he was going through some trouble in his marriage and his life. The expectations placed upon him and his marriage had caused the foundations around him to start cracking. My kids had known hardship, but this was truly something leading to destruction. One night or early morning, my husband's phone rang, which if you are a pastor you know is usually indicative of some tragedy. It was out of character for my husband, but he listened without telling me who it was or what it concerned. His own mother had recently suffered a stroke so I had already maintained that it concerned her. Then, he turned pale...and before I knew it he had jumped out of bed and was just about out the door. I begged for him to give me some kind of indication of the nature of the call before he left just for my own sanity! He told me our son had been in a accident but he was conscious and needed someone to come be with him. There were no words to express my concern and dismay. I began to get dressed to follow my husband to the hospital which was across town, in shock and terrified, praying and trusting God. I cried out "God, He's yours, always has been, you gave him to me, you know what you're doing. I don't understand this, but bring us peace and heal any part of my child's body that is injured". Soon, the phone rang as my husband told me not to come that he was being released. He had been in the hospital all night, unconscious for the most part, but in the MRI machine. The police had found him at an intersection in Atlanta, lying on the ground beside a crumbled jeep with a busted windshield and most of its contents scattered on Johnson Ferry Rd. He was alone, he had veered off the road and hit a light pole which was knocked down.

I went on to his house to prepare for him. In a while, he and his dad arrived back at his house, he was limping, nose broken, head wrapped, with sprains and fractures and groaning to go to bed. As I crawled up in the bed with my son, I smelled a foreign substance that sickened me. It was alcohol, but my son was not a drinker. He had preached for so many years against the use of drugs and alcohol in his youth gatherings and had never had the desire to use. Until now. I myself being a teetotaler at the time, was dismayed and confused by the turn of events. "Why?" I said, "what happened". "I don't know Mom,I guess I just got tired of the fight and tried to escape". "By hitting a phone pole?" "No" he said "by getting intoxicated". Oh, my heart sunk with such grief. The policeman on the site said that Britt should have been killed. He reported that when he walked up and saw the bible and study materials, along with a guitar strewn all over the street, he knew this was not your normal DUI. And when he talked to my son, he knew by his kindness and demeanor he was in turmoil and trauma. Thank God there was no permanent brain injury and after surgery he made a full recovery. But that was his place of "Peniel", the place where the man Jacob, "the deceiver" was when he wrestled an angel for his life. Not wanting to be changed into the man a God made him to be "Israel". "Peniel" literally means "the face of God", the concept being "I have seen God face to face and my life has been preserved". For reasons unknown to us, our son was fighting for his life. And it was crucial for him to make the right choices, the "God" choices. Ultimately, this whole "Peniel" experience led to my son's Salvation, restoration, and transformation!! It also served as a life changer for us, opening our eyes to the ravages of alcoholism and giving us a chance to receive much needed ministry!

Today my son is in his mid thirties and holds a rewarding job in the recovery community and has personally ministered to more people who would have previously been untouchable, but God knew just how and when to bed my son down and give him back his life!! And that tragic miracle led me on a higher path with God than I have ever known! Trust God, He is the maker, creator, and life giver. Not the manipulator, dictator and punisher. He will lead you to your Peniel and beyond!

"Yes, because God's your refuge, the High God your very own home, Evil can't get close to you, harm can't get through the door. He ordered his angels to guard you wherever you go. If you stumble, they'll catch you; their job is to keep you from falling. You'll walk unharmed among lions and snakes, and kick young lions and serpents from the path. "If you'll hold on to me for dear life," says God, "I'll get you out of any trouble. I'll give you the best of care if you'll only get to know and trust me. Call me and I'll answer, be at your side in bad times; I'll rescue you, then throw you a party. I'll give you a long life, give you a long drink of Salvation!"
Psalms 91:9-16 MSG

13 THE BED THAT CREATES LIFE

Life is a very important part of God's economy and divine balance. Just a side note here, we are told that "the life is in the blood" and that the blood cries out from the soil unto God. Medically, this is obvious. He might have made us of dirt and molded our flesh into his likeness, but blood is the life force. It courses through our veins providing the necessary nutrients for life. To shed your blood for something means you absolutely will give your life to make it so. Once all of our blood is drained we cease to exist. How many of you as a child, ever had a blood brother or sister? Someone who you were willing to prick your finger or inflict a small cut for? Someone you wanted to share blood with? When Jesus shed his blood, God finally shared blood with us. In the Old Testament "cutting covenant" meant that blood was involved in the covenant which made it a matter of life and death. The covenant that bound two people once cut, could not be broken. And a real covenant always involved blood.

A Jewish practice that illustrates this involves a bride and groom on their wedding day. After the marriage ceremony the bride waited for her groom who would be escorted to their "chuppah room" or honeymoon bed by a group of selected people who would wait outside the door in anticipation. Once the couple consummated, and the virgin gave herself to her husband, the sheet was then presented to the anxious group.

They would proceed to hang it on a pole and show the wedding party, that indeed the bride was a virgin saved for her husband and that indeed the covenant they had made at the alter was complete. Then the wedding celebration would commence! The sheet was kept for safe keeping by the bride herself. If there was no blood the woman was taken to the city gates and slain. As we can see this was a rather male dominated culture, but the woman was the special vessel whose womb was to carry new life. That was the meaning of covenant to the Jewish nation. It was serious business to remain a virgin, or your life could be taken. Because the spilled blood meant that a God considered the union valid. We don't have any such customs in today's world! Thank Jesus, He took care of it by shedding His own blood. But it does not lessen the importance that God places on procreation. And not only is human life sacred to God, He created and desires all living beings to be what He created them to be.

This concept hit home with me late one night or early morning when I was reading a book about the afterlife. A woman was conveying her experience as she was escorted through the portals to paradise. In her description of what she perceived to be Heaven, she described all the vivid colors she was seeing for the first time, and the trees and leaves of the trees and the sea of glass. I began focusing on the fact that there will be the same nature where God dwells as there is here only glorified and made pure, back to its original state, "the Lion will lay down with the Lamb". I've always loved nature, animals, sounds, smells. I believe there are healing powers God put in nature yet to be released. About that time I looked up to see a vision of a beautiful meadow, with a huge oak tree and animals such as deer and antelope wandering and grazing. I then heard crying as I felt myself, now transmuted into the vision, stepping on beautiful grass. I noticed a beautiful flower and I reached down to pluck it, and I felt sorrow in my bones. As this happened I suddenly became an extension of the flower, went down into the roots and back up the tree. All of my nerves were alive and tingling. Suddenly I heard a loud bang and saw a beautiful doe fall at the base of the trunk. Then somehow I knew God was crying. When I awoke from this state I immediately woke my husband and told him to help me remember that vision and that feeling. We are told that all creation praises God and obviously, they worship the sun...their source of life, by turning their faces and pedals to its light. God loves this Earth, and He wants us to care for it. Since this vision I have realized that we were told to be tenders of this Earth. I believe God was just showing me how all of nature, since man turned from the original creator, dies daily for our pleasure.

No, it's not wrong to walk on grass, or pluck a flower to bask in its glory, or hunt animals for food, but we must do it in an attitude of awe and wonder, that something always gives up its life for us to live and have pleasure.

As God breathed His Spirit into that first "dirt" man or earthen vessel, He rebreathes that same breath into us through nature. What a concept! Maybe the naturalists don't have it so wrong after all? Perhaps we need to begin to recognize the Spirit of love that works through nature. That to everything there is a season and purpose...even how we obtain our food from nature has become so diluted. We go to our grocery stores and eat our processed, pre-packaged food and never once have to remember the price being paid for that food to come to our table. Especially in America, we have forgotten the simplicity of living off of the land. Our children and grandchildren aren't even made aware of the fact that something gave it's life for them to consume their fast food hamburger, sandwich, or nuggets! How do we expect to reconnect with the God of the dirt...yes , He created with dirt, as a matter of fact we are only mere dirt, enlivened by His Spirit. One thing I've learned in being around people whose spirits have left their bodies is that it doesn't take long for that process of our bodies returning to dirt to begin. Once the last breath is breathed, an immediate decomposition begins to take place and we return to our "dirt" state. We are of this earth, we survive and receive sustenance from nature and this earth God placed us on and as those who will begin to "show forth" who God really is, we must return to the understanding and commitment to be kind to the earth. I'm not just speaking of "going green" that's important for our survival and clean existence, but I'm speaking of recognizing the importance in the process and cycle of life. We were all made to be intimately involved with nature, to somehow find a way to interact so that we appreciate from whence we came! And in that is great healing. Because of technology and the commercialization of the agricultural industry we seldom think about the price paid to produce our food. I believe this grieves the Creative Spirit of God. It's so sad that our children play games in which they easily obliterate some image of an animal or even another human being and find it thrilling! It's sad to me, when we simply hunt for sport instead of to accomplish a means to an end. It's our responsibility to harvest the earth, whether it be harvesting vegetables and fruit and grains, which is fulfilling our role in "subduing and tending" the earth placed upon us at creation, or to harvest meat to give sustenance, we have been given the role of "care-takers" of our earth and that includes pruning and sometimes culling the earth of the overpopulation of certain animals. But the sad thing is in making the taking of life a "sport" with no reward but the thrill to kill, in doing this, we take away the preciousness of God's provision for us. Not that we shouldn't hunt, fish or chase for sport, but when we do, we can display and restore an attitude of gratitude rather than pride and pleasure at taking life. It's in man to do it and can be very cathartic as we are allowed to take control of our own food sources and participate in tending the earth, but it's all about an attitude.

The activists who speak out against such things mean well, and awareness of the heinous and inhuman treatment of certain animals is very important, but God looks at the end result, the act of the heart. And His children will recognize the significance in revering life as if He Himself dwells there! It's a day for churches and followers of God, and lovers of life to become involved in a proper way in our own communities in how animals and natural resources are handled. The ones who desire God's heart will also be the ones who nurture and care for, and promote kindness and thankfulness in even the places we take for granted! We shouldn't be environmentalists, so to speak, just because it feels right and is the movement of the hour. We should be environmental heroes because it's our job, our ultimate role in this realm! Then we can begin to be restored and renewed and as the earth heals so will God's people. My encouragement is to get involved in your area of influence in helping keep others aware of how they affect nature for the positive or for the negative. And pray that God gives us wisdom.

Now here we come to a part oft times misunderstood and not even spoken about in certain circles until a few decades ago. Part of making a bed for someone and inviting them to be intimate with you, has to do with the enticements we use. Women are endowed with certain things that attract potential lovers, and so are men. In the bible we, the sons of God, the assembly, the church...are also referred to as "The Bride". As much as we can become uncomfortable with the concept, we are also created to achieve a spiritual intimacy with our maker. And as nature itself shows us and demonstrates to us, we see that as we employ our God given gifts, we are becoming more attractive to our lover. After all, the whole of life is simply a huge love story between a force...a Divine Being who only knows love, and the object of His affection, which is you and I. Let me qualify by saying, those of us who respond to Him, those who move by His touch, and are guided by His eyes, are easily excited by the whisper of His love and intentions, these are they who can take that divine love out of the "bedroom" so to speak, or the place of intimacy and become a channel through which to release more of the divine nature into a hurting world. This personal intimacy with God may include songs of passion and love, poems of the heart, spending time reading reflections of His heart in His word, meditating or daydreaming about His goodness and all of His glorious attributes and abilities. Falling in love is something as human beings that is elusive to us. For some reason there are things that lead up to that moment or significant time period when you know you have feelings of passionate love for another person. When you rehearse it, you remember feelings of warm acceptance, desires of having physical exchanges of affection, just being close to the person, or expressing yourself and your feelings for them. And when love between a man and woman begins to flourish it's very hard to conceal it. I'm not just speaking of infatuation, but I am speaking of that realization that overcomes you when you are aware that you will never be the same because this person has entered your life. When deep mature love comes into your life, you realize that it's not a whim, but it's there to stay. No matter where that person is, a part of you will always be with them. No matter how long it is between interactions, when you do interact, you are just as passionate about their persona and expressing your affection as you've ever been. You are occupied with thoughts of them, and even if the thoughts are not at the forefront of your mind, you know they are always there. The two of you share things that no one else would understand, you desire to serenade them with songs of love and hear their voice, know everything about them, and you long to be in their presence. Your main desire for the one you love with this depth is that they be happy and whole, that they are fulfilled in their dreams and hopes, that they are never lonely, and although you would like to be the one to help meet those needs, you also know that you could let go if you were standing in the way of that person's well-being. Love, real love that I speak of, never imposes, it has proper boundaries, always hoping the other person is comfortable, never degrading or doing anything that might offend them and their nature. I've been privileged to experience these things as have most of you. In the beginning of a relationship it's relatively easy to foster that love and feel it in an unbridled way. But as time passes you have to make decisions as to how this will affect your life. Will this be the person you forsake all else for and cleave to? And if that's not possible, in such cases, you must then make the decision of how to reconcile your emotions and your heart felt passions and negotiate them into the fabric of your own life. True love desires no hurt, although there might be initial pain in learning how to let go, when you love to this level you find a peace in knowing that you did the best thing for the welfare of the other person. Selfishness is not comfortable in this "bed" that we provide in which to nurture the love we are living.

We must provide a bed upon which love can rest, feel comfortable, and even become intimate enough with us to let down His guard and stay awhile. We can have no pretense. This group of people on planet earth, who we will call the "illuminated ones", will move to the touch and whims of their "lover" to use terms of the bedroom. And the only way to become trustworthy enough for our lover to come, make His bed, and stay with us, is by disciplining our own thoughts and motivations towards becoming one with Him. But this is not about morals, it is about attitude. An attitude that only the Author of the universe can script within a heart in times of sheer transparent vulnerability which leads to intimacy. Our Creator speaks to us in terms that all can hear and tune into, but our Lover speaks the word He Has already written upon our hearts. It's here, In this "bed" that we provide for Him...be it our devotion, meditation, or time of worship upon which we are instructed on how to be more like Him. It's here where we find heart, creativity, and even, life! I started with the bed because this is where everything really starts, literal bed or not, it's reveals the concept that we must give ourselves completely to Him to find who we really are...and in that giving we are transliterated into something others can read.

14 THE NEWLYWED BED AND THE WRITINGS OF LOVE

In our most recent societal mores, we have become so desensitized to the true meaning of physical intimacy that the concept of a virgin bride is lost to us. Jesus clearly indicates that one of his missions and commissions is to gather a Bride and many references are used in the Word concerning marriages, weddings, and relationships. Of course the Apostle Paul gives us a view of the marriage bed as being honorable and the bed not being defiled. He also speaks of how a man and a woman in a covenantal marriage are to treat one another saying:

"But this is the covenant that I will make with the house of Israel after those days, says the Lord:I will put My law in their minds, and write it on their hearts; and I will be their God, and they shall be My people."
Jer 31:33-34 NKJV

And this is so good translated in simpler terms. The purists who use no other version than the King James Bible may be missing out on the nuggets hidden for all humanity if we could decipher it for a better understanding. Men wrote the King James from the early manuscripts because old English was their language. As long as context and character are not damaged, we can justifiably explore more recent versions, such as this from the Message translation:

"This is the brand–new covenant that I will make with Israel when the time comes. I will put my law within them—WRITE it on their hearts!— and be their God. And they will be my people. They will no longer go around setting up schools to teach each other about God. They'll know me firsthand, the dull and the bright, the smart and the slow. I'll wipe the slate clean for each of them. I'll forget they ever sinned!"
Jeremiah 31:33-34 MSG

The emphasis is mine, he said he would "write" upon our hearts.

Written upon your hearts...have you ever thought about how God composes? In the Genesis we are told that God "spoke", literally He "sang" the universe into existence. There's little difference with God, He has orchestrated and composed everything with a purpose and destiny...not "destination". That includes mankind, He spoke us into existence, but the scripture says He will "write His law upon our hearts." But In order to write you must be "hands on".

The very first account of God writing is found when Moses meets God upon Mt. Moriah to receive the commandments for God's people to live by. In the story, God called Moses up to the mountain...after many different complicated qualifiers were achieved by the people (side note here, the law always complicates) and after giving the law verbally God tells Moses that He will "write" them upon tablets of stone. This word is a root word and basically means to "grave, or inscribe". So, taken literally, this would mean that somehow God used His hand to inscribe the images of His Word into stone tablets. What this story conjures up for me is the scene in the movie "Exodus" when Charleton Heston as Moses, stands amazed and a little scared as God flings down fire and invisibly engraves these words into two stone tablets! I'm not sure that's how it happened, but however it was done, God wanted Moses to be able to hold these words in his hand so he could instruct and teach and even show the others how to follow God's given laws. In our day of technology writing something, or sending an email is not quite as powerful as when someone takes the time and energy to sit down and write with paper and pen, words for someone else. But this depicts the serious nature by which God was delivering a part of Himself into the care of the people. And it was His attempt to keep them safe, bless them, help them along their way by the giving of these laws...all good things.

But, as of yet, He hadn't truly felt the flesh side of life. Something new happens when that takes place. But at this point God gives of Himself to the people by leaving a mark...or an inscription signifying unto them His law and His ordinances. Of course Moses let a temper tantrum over the foolish folly of the people lead him to destroy the first two tablets, so God graciously wrote them out again. Sounds familiar doesn't it? Ever had someone lovingly break the tablets of the law over your head...as some Christians do when they get angry? the first thing they want to do with someone they disagree with or they are angry with or even haven't taken the time to understand, is to get out the tablets of the law and break them over their heads!! We see it all the time and we hear, "well, the bible says..." and yes the bible addresses a lot of things about the way we conduct ourselves, but when it is used to oppress others, it is almost as if we are taking those tablets in an angry rage and cracking them over the heads of those we are fed up with. We have little tolerance at times for those who don't believe the way we do, and I don't speak of tolerance in the sense of "accepting just anything". I'm talking of allowing others the same opportunity God gives each of us when coming into the knowledge of the Lord as "God". He gives much mercy, and usually it is a gradual process by which He teaches His children and always with much grace.

Everyone is on a different journey, they have their own path to follow and although we try to set up a standard whereby others see our beliefs, trying to impose upon and rush someone into an understanding never works. Validity is not gained in a bigger show of muscle. This is exactly the tactics that religious radicals and zealots use...the strategy of being forceful, the thought process of "we know the truth and if they don't see it, we'll make them see it"! Just remember that delivering God's word as truth doesn't require a whole lot of screaming, yelling, bantering, or fussing. In my opinion, this just shows our lack of confidence in our message. The truth is when we become people who are so intimate with the God of the Word... we will begin to understand that God is still speaking. And the true Word of God is not only written on our hearts but alive and powerful and sharp in itself. It doesn't need us to do anything but deliver it. We simply need to live by the compass and blue print God, our lover has written and laid down in our hearts. It is our gain to know His word, to know biblical truths, but God's Word is in us written there on a tablet of flesh, and the story never ends. My Lord, Christ is never ending and isn't contained by the limitations of time...He has already been where you're going. He sees you in the life of an eternal existence, and that life that radiates within us, is the Word written on our hearts. And this is just one way our intimacy with God reveals to us the plans He has for humanity.

"For I know the thoughts that I think toward you, says the Lord, thoughts of peace and not of evil, to give you a future and a hope."
Jer 29:11 NKJV

Lets take a look at that passage as it is translated in the "Message Bible".

"I know what I'm doing. I have it all planned out—plans to take care of you, not abandon you, plans to give you the future you hope for. "When you call on me, when you come and pray to me, I'll listening. "When you come looking for me, you'll find me."Yes, when you get serious about finding me and want it more than anything else, when you call on me, when you come and pray to me, I'll listen. "When you come looking for me, you'll find me. "Yes, when you get serious about finding me and want it more than anything else, I'll make sure you won't be disappointed."
Jer 29:11-13 MSG

15 WRITTEN BY THE LIGHT

Its a concept far beyond us to imagine how God takes laws once written on stone tablets, inscribed there, and converts them into a spiritual form which is alive for all eternity and then places them upon or into fleshly hearts of men. We know this process is not a literal writing upon a mass of tissue, it is a process unknown to us, but perfected by God. We can't understand it any more than we can understand how a man becomes spiritually "born again". I had a dear friend contact me recently about a co-worker who was intent on disproving the existence of God. Almost like Nicodemus asking "how can these things be?" He challenged my friend to have the "courage" to watch a debate debunking God, which in essence flies in the face of anything other than that which digresses man back to the origin of a mere ameba, and gives no place to anything other than what is visible. The invisible is all around us, the world runs by invisible properties. I don't understand gravity's properties anymore than you do...I'm sure many more brilliant than I feel they have mastered the explanation as to why gravity exists. But, not to stir up the apologetic dander that often accompanies this kind of thought, how are they sure it exists if they can't see it? We can witness the effects of this law that governs our secure existence on this planet, but you can't feel it or touch it, it just "is", did it all just chaotically come into order? Or how did it happen? In the Old Testament God challenges the man Job who had some questions of his own about the "whys" of his life.

"The question is, 'How can mere mortals get right with God?' If we wanted to bring our case before him, what chance would we have? Not one in a thousand! God's wisdom is so deep, God's power so immense, who could take Him on and come out in one piece? He moves mountains before they know what's happened, flips them on their heads on a whim. He gives the earth a good shaking up, rocks it down to its very foundations. He tells the sun, 'Don't shine,' and it doesn't; He pulls the blinds on the stars. All by himself He stretches out the heavens and strides on the waves of the sea. He designed the Big Dipper and Orion, the Pleiades and Alpha Centauri. We'll never comprehend all the great things He does; his miracle-surprises can't be counted. Somehow though He moves right in front of me, I don't see him; quietly but surely He's active, and I miss it."
Job 9:2-11 MSG

Job had a dilemma we will never have. He was tested by God without an advocate, or lawyer to fight for him. God gave us Jesus Christ who can now easily explain to God why we feel the way we feel and do the things we do. We are in a fortunate spiritual age! And God will not give us more than we can bear, He knows what He equipped us with to handle our challenges more than we do. Sometimes I surprise myself by what I can endure, but I shouldn't be surprised because my creator and Father knows just how much I can take. He knows that much better than I do.

But we must remember that we can only see as far as the light allows. In other words, we can never blame God if we encounter a place of confusion or doubt, or insecurity. Our condition is most probably the result of something being out of the scope of His illumination. He can't burn out and the light of His glory never diminishes, so the closer we get and the more we train our eyes to see by the Word, through faith, by the practice of His love, the more we have revealed to us. Oftentimes, a matter that has been so unresolved can be made clear and resolved in an instance once we come to an already existing light and step into it, and the best way to do this, to find answers to intimate questions is in intimate times with Him. And even if there's not an exact clarification, there will be the peace of knowing "it's all good" because the light we were made to live and show forth as a reflector, is the only place where true peace and revelation now reside. And it is a "peace that passes all understanding." So we can only attain the peace that our creator is leading us to as we enter this intimate rest. "You shall be led forth with peace".

A story I often convey to help illuminate this truth is something that occurred to me one day after the sudden death of my beloved sister. In our earthly relationship as sisters, Becky, had been my confidante through out my life. One morning I was in prayer over some situations happening in the church I pastored. I was walking around, proclaiming the victory and verbally crying out to God. When suddenly I got quiet enough to hear a voice. It was my sister's voice saying, "Rosie (a name only she would call me) stop striving, just step into the light." This came totally unexpected and out of the blue. I was listening for some loud proclamation from heaven or even for the phone to ring and for someone on the line to give me a "Word from The Lord"...a prophetic word concerning my situation. But instead I hear a voice that got my undivided attention! It was almost as if she was in the room with me it was so resonant. My immediate thinking was, "how in the world did my sister get back here from eternity?" I looked around the house and there it was again, a second time! "Rosie, don't cry, just step back into the light so you can see what to do". Suddenly from a window there appeared a soft shaft of light. The kind I would look at with amazement as a child and watch the particle of dust floating down while reflecting the sun's light. So I just put a foot over in It, looking around to see something, and, wow, it felt good, so I walked completely into the shaft and suddenly I lit up! My skin became an amber color, I felt a radiating warmth that I can only describe as...entering a hot tub with aching muscles. But I didn't have to acclimate to this heat, I immediately felt at peace! And I just basked in the warmth of the moment, no sound, nothing. And then I heard, in my heart...not Becky's voice this time, "here's your answer, here in My presence". It hit me that the answers exist already In the light that knows no time and cannot be stopped except for obstacles we might place in it's way! That beam began to stretch out of my family room and into my foyer area, stretching, not moving, but growing and expanding until it dissipated. But it hadn't really gone, it had now infused my heart with peace, knowledge and understanding. I didn't know the answers to my questions immediately, but what I did know is that when I got to a critical point of having to deal with those issues, this light that reveals truth would be available in me and grant me the ability to address them with wisdom. Which is exactly what happened. Not only did the problems in my congregation resolve, but the next Sunday we began experiencing a presence of peace in our church we had never known. Whether Becky actually spoke those words or the Holy Spirit used her voice to minister a truth to me that I might not have otherwise understood as His comfort, I don't know, but I do know that truth was infused to me. And I did my best to continue not only reflecting the light but giving it a larger space in my life by resigning all worries to it.

Of course I believe this to be Jesus Christ, who at His coming said "I am the light of the world"! And He continues to be that for me. I sometimes wander out of this glorious light provided to me, but when I do, and recognize it, I immediately ask the Spirit of truth who will "guide us into all truth", to put me back in the path. It's sort of like what happens to me sometimes at night while driving. As I age, I have difficulty seeing in the dark and being sure that what I'm seeing is really there, or in my imagination! I watch carefully for the illuminated lane markings so I can stay between them, here where I live in Tennessee are many back roads with very little light. But when I put on my bright lights...everything that can be illuminated is made evident and suddenly I can see the turn ahead, or the sign ahead or the biker whose vest and helmet are reflecting my lights, or the eyes of a raccoon or deer that I'm approaching. Thank goodness for that, It's brilliant that God gave animals built in light reflectors, that show up in the light. My point is, if you're not in a position for the light to shine out of you and to illuminate all the sign posts and the eyes of what's in your path, you are definitely going to encounter many unnecessary consequences. It's a glorious thing when we can finally relinquish everything to the light of God and stop striving to see in the dark!!

Returning to the subject of how God writes upon us...I chose to bring three times that this happened in scripture to your attention. As I said the first time was when He wrote the law on tablets for Moses...twice! The Second is when he wrote upon the wall for the king in the story of Nebuchadnezzar. In the book of Daniel a very interesting story unfolds.

16 GOD'S FINGERS

"In the same hour the fingers of a man's hand appeared and wrote opposite the lamp stand on the plaster of the wall of the king's palace; and the king saw the part of the hand that wrote. Then the king's countenance changed, and his thoughts troubled him, so that the joints of his hips were loosened and his knees knocked against each other."

I admit as a child I would try with all my might to imagine those fingers. They are described as the fingers of a man's hand. Notice, we are told this wall was illuminated and Nebuchadnezzar was able to see what was written. However, because it was only illuminated by the light of the lamp and not the spiritual light of knowledge and understanding the meaning remained a mystery! When the queen offered to get Daniel to read this it was because he had so much light within him that he could see what other's couldn't, she described him as having "light and understanding" or intellectual brilliance. Now I'm not splitting hairs here, but God wrote it, it was there plain to see, but the meaning was not revealed to anyone but a man who could see it illuminated in the divine light. I am under the conviction that the Holy Spirit and the light are inseparable and Jesus Christ came to bring this light, but as already stated, Jesus told his followers after His death before His ascension this: "it is not for you to know times or seasons which the Father has put in His own authority, but you shall receive power after the Holy Spirit has come upon you...and you Shall BE..." We need not strive when this light, the Holy Spirit who show us "all things" illuminates everything concerning our lives. He is described as "the comforter", etc most of which are attributed in one way or another to Light. Jesus was sent to be the light, but then He sent back the light in a form that all men could apprehend simply by asking!! And in the book of Acts they did receive, and the light divided and fell on each one of them individually, but it was the same light source.

What's so interesting here is that each person of that 120 people who showed up to wait and receive this promise, experienced the light working through them in a different way. They all spoke with tongues, but in languages the people within ear shot could understand. And there was a conglomeration of people from many different nationalities in Jerusalem at that time. This engenders so much hope within me. The Holy Spirit of God present and alive inside of me keeps me on the track of truth and transforms itself to move and work through me according to whatever challenge a situation presents! I could easily expound on this but if we "stay in the light as he is in the light" we know that wherever we are will be where we are destined to be. And whatever we do, no matter how small or how large it may seem to us, it's God's work, and nothing that is God's work is small!! So, again, all we need to do is "be".

But don't think for a moment that you ever arrive at the "being" stage only to sit back on your laurels and just be lazy. We are given this story by the apostle:

"There was a man sent from God, whose name was John. This man came for a witness, to bear witness of the Light, that all through him might believe. He was not that Light, but was sent to bear witness of that Light. That was the true Light which gives light to every man coming into the world. He was in the world, and the world was made through Him, and the world did not know Him. He came to His own, and His own did not receive Him. But as many as received Him, to them He gave the right to become children of God, to those who believe in His name: who were born, not of blood, nor of the will of the

flesh, nor of the will of man, but of God."
Jn 5:9-13

So we are still being transformed daily, and "becoming" like the light, which was Christ and now is His Holy Spirit within those who believe in His name. It's interesting to me, and reveals the workings of this process, that in previous verses that John says of himself... that he was sent to "bear witness" of that light, but he was not that light. Why couldn't John be the light of God? He was created for it just like we are, in God's image and endowed with the same Spiritual breath...because John preceded the ability given when the Holy Spirit was sent back to us by the Savior of mankind, the King of light, the light Himself because Jesus was God. So even though before the advent of Christ, man was still made by love in order to produce this love and to show this love, because of man's mistake in the garden...or as I said earlier, his mistake at the place of creation. The mistake of relinquishing his spiritual God likeness, by taking it upon himself to circumvent God and try to rule his own life, he had lost touch with the light. He had become a vessel of dishonor...a cracked pot!!

When the serpent tempted the woman he told her that by eating of the fruit that God specifically forbade them to eat, she would be like God, knowing or perceiving good and evil. They thought that seeing like God saw would be incredible, until they gained the insight that some knowledge is better left unknown! They didn't need to know they were naked, they didn't need to ever know the pains of labor or of having to work out their salvation. They didn't and weren't created to reflect and know the deception of the deceiver. All the pains and woes and heartaches in this world came about as a result of our desire for something better than God. All we had to do was be!!! He would take care of the rest, now we have to labor for our food and shelter, and in having children in aging and dying. But before that wrong step that Adam and Eve took, we would have never ever had to deal with things God never intended for us to see! I realize this leaves the theological dispute about good and evil all kinds of back doors and escapes, but because my intention is to speak about the process of mankind "becoming" sons of God, I'll leave it there.

We can see in the Old Testament how the light would break through on occasion whether it was through a man or a woman attuned to receive it. Need I give examples? I won't start with examples because I am focusing on the new plan. The plan extended to us, the new policy, if you will, because when Jesus came as God, He did away with how we use to access the light...which was with bloodshed, sacrifice, and even begging. None of that is necessary because once we come into Christ and His Holy Spirit comes into us, we no longer need anything. The becoming process begins and all things begin to work together for our good. And we only need to continue in our love for Christ to receive all the benefits thereof. And however you believe that the Holy Spirit enters and interacts with us is irrelevant, just so we allow the Holy Spirit to enter our life by asking and then we can have that Divine illumination lighting our path...even His Word...written on the page and on our heart lights up under our feet to carry us on the ordered path. The path that God ordered the day He made us.

In the sense that God designed everything for a very particular function, we are designed and equipped to perfect specifications just as the birds of the air are equipped with a map on their brains to help them navigate in flight, we'll speak more about this later, but my point is, if God cared enough about this tiny bird to equip it with a map by which to fly so it wouldn't be confused, then how much treasure must He have deposited in our earthen vessels to assist us in accomplishing our job? For Jesus said, "of how much more value are you than the bird?"

17 WRITING OUR DEFENSE

The third time I'll call to your attention concerning God's handwriting, is when Jesus walked among us and was in defense of the sinner, the prostitute...writing in the sand....! Thank God for this showcase of God's unimaginable love for us. Jesus, in the temple is met by a group of people shuffling around to vindicate the law. They have a young girl in their clutches and are preparing to dispense with her by lifting their stones of accusation, literally, hurling them at her and watching the life God gave her be crushed out.

"Now early in the morning He came again into the temple, and all the people came to Him; and He sat down and taught them. Then the scribes and Pharisees brought to Him a woman caught in adultery. And when they had set her in the midst, they said to Him, "Teacher, this woman was caught in adultery, in the very act. Now Moses, in the law, commanded us that such should be stoned. But what do You say?" This they said, testing Him, that they might have something of which to accuse Him. But Jesus stooped down and wrote on the ground with His finger, as though He did not hear. So when they continued asking Him, He raised Himself up and said to them, " He who is without sin among you, let him throw a stone at her first."
And again He stooped down and wrote on the ground. Then those who heard it, being convicted by their conscience, went

out one by one, beginning with the oldest even to the last. And Jesus was left alone, and the woman standing in the midst. When Jesus had raised Himself up and saw no one but the woman, He said to her, " Woman, where are those accusers of yours? Has no one condemned you?"
She said, "No one, Lord."
And Jesus said to her, " Neither do I condemn you; go and sin no more."
Then Jesus spoke to them again, saying, " I am the light of the world. He who follows Me shall not walk in darkness, but have the light of life"
Jn 8:2

No man has the authority to be the "law enforcer" in deed or attitude. Even God Himself, in the form of a man, wouldn't judge this young lady. Sure, the fault was plain to see. She had been caught in the act! Now put whatever "act" you want to here. It could just as well have been the act of "lying, cheating, stealing, coveting, hurting another, concealing truth, manipulating with emotional tyranny, unforgiveness" just to mention a few. But this woman's "act" was of a baser element, she was an adulterer. This action constituted the participation of another and though she was not alone in her "act", she was the one who "seemed" more guilty. We assume this woman was a prostitute, but it's not made clear. I'd like to take a moment here to express something revealed to me in a very graphic way. Recently, my husband and I have had our eyes opened to the treachery of the sex slave trade all around us. Just in the city in which we live, there are organizations working around the clock to free those who have been enslaved willingly or unwillingly by a sub culture in our society who find it easy to use the suffering and needs of other human beings to make a profit for themselves, especially with women and children. It starts out somewhere in a poor village, or in an indigent community, or in a broken family which has provided little to no stability for their children. And it ends up in a brothel or an illegal massage parlor or hidden in the dark rooms of a seedy motel. Sometimes it began by a simple act of desperation for food and clothing and shelter, a parent who can't provide for a child who is told that there is someone who can provide a better life for their child and even for themselves if they would only release them into the care of people who could put them to work for an allotted amount of time. What parent wouldn't desire more for their child? And sometimes men and women who are looking for the opportunity to make money themselves, who don't have an honest education or skill of any kind, stuck themselves in the desperation of human need, will solicit these women and children and offer them up for sex to meet their own needs. Or, God forbid, they take them, literally snatch them off of the streets and put them in a ring of prostituted hell. These victims have no one to help them, nowhere to turn, no recourse except to obey their captors, but it's plain to see who is at fault here or is it? Do we condemn someone for needing food and clothing and shelter? No, but we do condemn those who instead of begging off of society, take it into their own hands to do what can be done for survival, especially if it means they must sell their bodies? Notice in the story of this woman thrown down like refuse to be stoned to death, that she alone was under scrutiny and judgment. There was no true judge or jury to give her a chance to explain herself. She was simply a casualty in the ever so common societal legalistic jungle. Her conspirator was nowhere to be seen. She, alone, was being judged for not only the misdeed of the man involved, but of the misdeeds of every man, woman, and child, alive.

We have all been caught in this societal trap. And what is frowned upon in one culture is mainstream in another. That's why the only standard we can actualize is the one written upon our hearts, by our Creator, the one Being who actually knows what's good and bad for us, and then brings it to light by His Holy Spirit. Jesus was the depiction of God in action here. He didn't declare that what this woman had done shouldn't be considered "sin", He merely brought into focus the reality that everyone falls into the category of falling short of the standard of the law! His action and reaction showcased a God who understood man's capacity for need and desperation. Yes, the written law was breached, but Jesus simultaneously puts several things in perspective for us.

First, He doesn't jump to a conclusion. The religious leaders are so gleefully expecting this man of love to be caught in the vice of the Mosaic law. Their expectations are met with what could be misconstrued as indifference. But in actuality, Jesus was writing His own law of love in the sand. I can't say for sure what it read. But I see here an act of love, stopping to ponder and consider the ramifications of the situation before just jumping to a "ruling" that was written on breakable tablets. Jesus was rewriting the Law and purpose of God for this life...and this would become a gift to every man.

As they continued to ask Him and not let it go we are told that Jesus "raised himself up". Could this be symbolic of what He knew was on the horizon for humanity? He knew that God Almighty was preparing to lay down the ultimate sacrifice to once and for all abolish the law that had held humanity hostage. He "raised up" as if to say, "okay, fellas, look at Me, give Me your attention, I will show you the way through this." He knew the law better than anyone having been present when God forged it into stone. But now Jesus forges it into the changing sands of time in order to show this pinnacle of truth.

Jesus was in the business of not just being God here on this terra firma, or simply showing us how God would behave in dealing with all of life's challenges. But He came to rip the veil between humanity's misconceptions and God's absolutes. Love is an absolute because God is love. Love is really all that exists and everything else is either a reflection of it or a distortion of it. Hate is not the absence of love, but a distortion of it. The same is true of greed, and lust and covetousness, and actions against our brother are only the fruit of distorted love, which comes from one of these emotions. In the course of Christ's daily dose of miracles, nothing is done out of any other motivation.

Secondly, When Jesus writes upon the sand, He does it not only as a proclamation to those standing around, and to all humanity, but He is also making a written declaration of His intentions to forgive. All of heaven, and hell, were watching His every move and as His light penetrated all the places of human arrogance and ego, displayed in this story by the religious leaders, his light was burning away the thin line that separates the impossible from the possible. The Law made it impossible to love, it was not an expression of Agape love. It came out of a cosmic need to control disobedience and rebellion against the light of life. Yes the "light of life". Jesus raises up to say "I am the true light" because He is showing the reality of love and not the distortion we see through the law. And this is the same thing that happened at Calvary. He said "if I be lifted up, I will draw all men unto Me"...because there hanging on the cross, He would advertise the specialty of God. This was the ultimate sacrifice of love, laying down your own life so that another might live. And as He was raised into the light of the sun, which burned by his own power, He once again, showed that love overcomes and love wins!! It's that simple, yet that profound.

We try so hard to distort the truth of love in our lives, society, and our daily rituals. The bottom line is it all comes down in the end to you and your essence, how much you loved on this earth is congruent to how much love you have when you take leave for eternity. Because in the next realm there will be nothing but love. We won't be able to exist outside of love. so whatever in our lives was not of love will be burned up in the daylight of truth, the presence of God. It will be burned away like chaff being blown away. Our enemy, Lucifer or Satan, the evil one, however you may picture this evil force, is the father of distortion. He has made it his job to use smoke and mirrors to skew our perceptions and vision. If we walk in truth, in the light, in love, as He, Jesus is in the light, we not only see one another as God sees them, but we can only then have true fellowship. That's my level of love meeting your level of love. The God in me recognizing the God in you and relating to Him. Hatred and lust and their cousins are almost palpable. When someone is operating under distortion and the father of lies is working through their lives, the feelings associated and produced from it are almost tangible. I've felt it many times as I'm sure all of you have. In the presence of a truly evil person, your hair stands on end, you feel threatened, you feel danger. And on a smaller scale, when someone is being cruel or murderous in word or in deed, you also can feel that sick feeling associated with it.

People in many circles believe that there is no literal "hell". But we can't be sure what happens to those who die in their own distorted states, so foreign to who God is. They cannot dwell with Him because of their darkness...their is no light of love, therefore no light of life in them. But I propose that perhaps when they cross into eternity, that the light of love burns away the distortions, if you will. That which cannot continue on will be put to death in the light of truth and reality. It's inescapable....the fire that will burn must be painful. Would a God who is love allow this? He can't not allow it, He is love, He is light, darkness will evaporate in His presence one way or another. I know this to be so true by experiences I've had with those nearing death's door. They begin to see the truth of love. If they haven't yet accepted that Jesus is Lord, they slip into an unknown dimension, which most certainly is governed by all that is true, which is love. It's my conviction after having been with many who have passed, that once they truly receive and acknowledge the truth of the one and only Christ, that immediately any distortion, which can also be called transgressions against God's truth, or "sin", is burned away! They have walked into that Glorious light which sets all things in order, the light which envelopes with warmth and healing and peace.

If we come to that door having not lived a life in truth, which cannot be accomplished apart from truth, we are then cast into the outer darkness of chaotic distortion and the business of our continuing on is in question. What state would we continue on in? If there is no truth besides his love, then as the light abolishes the darkness, we are no longer there. The only thing that will live on are the qualities of God, not distortion. The distorted will be no more!! So much of scripture bears this out. We know that "the gift of God is eternal life through Jesus Christ"...yes we all have eternal life, but the quality of that life is dependent on our view of Jesus Christ, and how we have allowed His light to work in and through us. When the rich young ruler asks the question of Jesus, "what must I do to gain eternal life?" Jesus plunges headlong into a dissertation about charitable actions. He first tells him to obey the given law and commandments, and though He came to abolish the law, He here, clarifies that the part dealing with how we treat ourselves and others is what will be put under the light of judgment. He gives a series of parables and pictures instructing us how we should be living and then goes into this in Matthew,

"When the Son of Man comes in His glory, and all the holy angels with Him, then He will sit on the throne of His glory. All the nations will be gathered before Him, and He will separate them one from another, as a shepherd divides his sheep from the goats. And He will set the sheep on His right hand, but the goats on the left. Then the King will say to those on His right hand, 'Come, you blessed of My Father, inherit the kingdom prepared for you from the foundation of the world: for I was hungry and you gave Me food; I was thirsty and you gave Me drink; I was a stranger and you took Me in; I was naked and you clothed Me; I was sick and you visited Me; I was in prison and you came to Me. Then the righteous will answer Him, saying, 'Lord, when did we see You hungry and feed You, or thirsty and give You drink? When did we see You a stranger and take You in, or naked and clothe You? Or when did we see You sick, or in prison, and come to You?' And the King will answer and say to them, 'Assuredly, I say to you, inasmuch as you did it to one of the least of these My brethren, you did it to Me.' Then He will also say to those on the left hand, 'Depart from Me, you cursed, into the everlasting fire prepared for the devil and his angels: for I was hungry and you gave Me no food; I was thirsty and you gave Me no drink; I was a stranger and you did not take Me in, naked and you did not clothe Me, sick and in prison and you did not visit Me.' Then they also will answer Him, saying, 'Lord, when did we see You hungry or thirsty or a stranger or naked or sick or in prison, and did not minister to You?' Then He will answer them, saying, 'Assuredly, I say to you, inasmuch as you did not do it to one of the least of these, you did not do it to Me.' And these will go away into everlasting punishment, but the righteous into eternal life."
Mat. 25:21-46

Does love not save the day here? Is it not obvious that what Jesus conveys is that He is looking for those who operate by love and who live this out in deed? He also shows, in the case of the rich young ruler, that He's interested more in the motivation of true charity and the passion to act in someone else's interest rather than just the deeds reciprocated by the law. This lays down for us our whole life's purpose.

People go about aimlessly seeking their "callings" and "purpose for living" when, plainly Jesus has shown us that we simply exist to operate in and demonstrate who God really is, love. We are not here by happenstance or by default, or any other reason than just to be God to this earth. To heal the earth and its inhabitants, to shed light, show love, and abolish darkness in so doing. And each of us is born a vessel of honor to be filled with the Glory of his pre-imminence. As we are given a set of giftings, whether we see it by heredity or not, He has built into us the stuff we are made of, the necessary talents and abilities we will ever need have to accomplish this task. And our destiny is to be enveloped back into Him, back into the light to rule the many universes and all of creation with Him. We are original pieces of His life made by His own doing...out of the Trinity of Father, Son, and Holy Ghost, the only three parts of His unfathomable Being He has chosen to reveal to us! In the light this is crystal clear. The people who will rule and reign with God will be those who "overcome" this present condition to reveal God, and Jesus illuminated the path we must follow to accomplish this. The third thing being revealed in this story is how "hands on" God really is and wants us to be. in the book of the Revelation of John, we are told that He will Himself wipe away the tears from our eyes.
He's a hands on God but now He chooses to use human hands through which to work. This is why touching others brings a warmth, healing and love that nothing else can, it's a different kind of intimacy. It's a proven scientific fact that there is power in the human touch. When a person is distressed or ill, even critically ill, the touch of another human being brings comfort, love, healing. People who are hugged everyday are much healthier than those who are not. We need to surround ourselves with a community of love so we can stay close to God's touch. This is one operation the church, the true living, breathing church, will provide, the transport of God's love into the lives around them by their touch. The laying on of hands holds a significant power. A power that cannot be substituted with anything else. Holding someone when they are distraught, or sick or dying improves their chances of coming to health.

There are those who specifically know how to bring God's touch to humanity. Those in the medical field have a particularly privileged opportunity to practice this. I remember reading when the Aids epidemic was first coming to light, that because of the mystery surrounding it's ability to spread, medical personnel and those who came in contact with those infected were encouraged to protect themselves against the disease. It was dictated that gloves should be worn during any interaction with these patients. I read the story of one young man who said that he was desperately ill and felt he was slipping away. The nurse with him was working to reduce his fever and keep him comfortable. But she did something strange which was considered a risk of one's own life, when she took off her gloves to hold his hand. He said it had been so long since he'd felt the "warmth" of the human touch. The warmth generated by compassion and flowing directly from the light of life Himself. You see, this warmth of love comes when true compassion is activated in the human spirit. This man begin to respond to the medication and ultimately lived. His spirit rallied to the warmth of love. A compassionate "God" touch had saved his life. Babies devoid of human touch become sick, unfeeling, and dry up. It is a fact that our touch brings positive outcomes. But imagine the force of God's touch and then imagine the power in our touch to Him. What can be generated when we touch others as ministering unto God? Let's look at a story and maybe see something different this time.

"While He spoke these things to them, behold, a ruler came and worshiped Him, saying, 'My daughter has just died, but come and lay Your hand on her and she will live.' So Jesus arose and followed him, and so did His disciples. And suddenly, a woman who had a flow of blood for twelve years came from behind and touched the hem of His garment. For she said to herself, 'If only I may touch His garment, I shall be made well.' But Jesus turned around, and when He saw her He said, 'Be of good cheer, daughter; your faith has made you well.' And the woman was made well from that hour. When Jesus came into the ruler's house, and saw the flute players and the noisy crowd wailing, He said to them, 'Make room, for

the girl is not dead, but sleeping.' And they ridiculed Him. But when the crowd was put outside, He went in and took her by the hand, and the girl arose. And the report of this went out into all that land."
Mat 9:18-26 NKJV

The woman who touched Jesus in this story did something critical...she activated love's ability. Her faith, or the belief in the substance of things not seen, the impossible things, led her to reach out and touch Him. And although Jesus doesn't say "your touch had made you whole", he says your "faith has made you whole", it was the actual putting faith in an action by touching Him that released his power to heal. Then He goes into a dead girl and touches her by taking her hand. Could it be that this woman's faith actually released even the power for Jesus to raise the dead? Oh, I like to think so. Being raised and serving primarily in a "Charismatic" ministry, I have witnessed and heard of many great healings through the laying on of hands. I have been the recipient and the administrator in many many situations. But when I was in my twenties I had a brush with the divine in a man that was to forever change my life.

Oral Roberts, known as one of the greatest ministers of healing in the Charismatic Movement came to visit our church. I had experienced healing on many occasions through mere prayer and faith. But something different occurred to me when I encountered this man's touch. I had been suffering from severe migraine headaches for years. They were so bad that at the mere onset of the visual aura if I don't go to bed I would be deathly sick. I was still sick, stuck in bed for days, but if I didn't disengage from life and rest in a cold, dark, room...I would be sick for weeks. I sang with the worship team at the church at that time and this was a special service during a conference that we had been preparing for with Bro. Roberts. I also worked on the church staff and I remember having been so sick all day and afternoon that I couldn't do my job interviewing and doing on camera promos and shoots for the television program which I hosted for the ministry. There was no way I could see to drive or even get dressed to attend the service. So I called my dad, who was the senior pastor to deliver the bad news of my condition and told him I didn't think it was possible for me to participate. I had two children who were all too familiar with seeing their mother under the assault of gut wrenching pain and nausea. I knew I would have to get them dressed and fed and take them with me as well. My husband also worked on staff and was in charge of publishing and involved with much of the media process. He also had responsibilities at the conference and was at the church preparing for the service. It grieved me beyond measure to miss out on something we had all looked so forward to. When I made the call, my dad was resting in preparation of the night ahead. When I told him of the headache, he took in a deep breath and said, "well baby doll, you know what you're capable of better than I do, but if you can push through, it would be beneficial I think to you and I really wanted you to meet Bro. Roberts." At the time, I had met just about anyone and everyone who was known as a leader in Christendom. To be quite honest, it didn't hold a lot of bargaining power with me to get to meet someone else. But I thought better of giving up and decided to rally and press on. I couldn't see well, so I barely was able to reapply any makeup, which was very little at the time, and I wasn't sure about my hair...but in true warrior fashion, I got on the dress I was to wear and proceeded to get the kids ready to leave. When I got to the car, I realized I couldn't see to drive, but my options were limited. I told my son, who was nine or ten years old that Mama was having a headache. I told him I was going to drive very slowly but he would have to help me with the red lights and where other cars were located around me. It was about a twelve minute drive to the church and with his help, during some agonizing bouts of fighting the nausea, and creeping every mile, we made it. Some kind person greeted me at my parking space to help me and the kids in and we made our way up to my dad's office to find out service details. As I walked in, it occurred to me how ironic it was that I was about to walk into the presence of the greatest faith healer of our time battling with what seemed like a demonic sickness. This man had seen blinded eyes open, the deaf hear, cancer healed, the lame walk and even the dead raised so I wasn't about to complain with my malady that paled in comparison! So, I did what came naturally and put on my happy, well, and energetic face, which was my companion through many hard things and became my method of survival.

Bro.Oral Roberts was taller than I had thought him to be and he and my Dad were talking as I walked in. My Daddy saw me slip in and immediately called attention to me by saying "you made it"! After that pronouncement he then introduced me to Bro. Roberts who took one look in my eyes and said "little Lady, I'm so glad you pushed through, your faith is going to make you whole!" He said "is it ok if I pray for you?" "Please!" I said. He took my head in his big warm hands and turned my face up to look him in the eyes. This is when he called me "little Beth" not because I was so little, but I surmised he could see my helpless deportment as the facade I thought I had so masterfully employed had now crumbled at his feet. He said "little Beth, I want you to understand what's happening here. I'm coming into agreement with you in the heavenly places over your healing, once I do that, I will not come out of agreement with you as long as I live." It then hit me the gravity of this matter. My life was about to be altered forever from a brush with divine energy and power. I felt the sensation of a warm hand on my head right where the pain was, and he said "I command our sister be released from this grip of pain!". Immediately as he made an action of release, the pain just dissipated and the nausea was gone. I was actually hungry! He put one hand on either side of my head and cupped my face and lifted my eyes up to meet his. And he said "it's gone isn't it?" With tears wetting his hands I said "yes"! Then he said, "I feel that this will be a daily walk of faith for you...God has deposited the gift of healing in you". Notwithstanding, I was and am aware that same power is resident in anyone who believes in the healing power of love. However when he said this I knew he foresaw the pain of having such a gift. The gift to actually match people's faith in Christ for their healing. But it takes a vessel that can be poured through to release this healing. No, it doesn't demand perfection or spiritual purity or sanctification, necessarily. It simply takes willingness.

Then I remembered while at a Kathryn Khulman service at the age of thirteen, praying for the ability to heal the sick and hurting. The problem with this or the phenomenon associated with it is that if the vessel is poured through sometimes that vessel must understand how much compassion is warranted for faith to actually ignite over a person's need. Very often, the flesh that houses the gift of healing will itself experience the pain of sickness. This man Oral Roberts was himself healed of tuberculosis early in his life. He stood on his feet so many hours at a time, and used his hands so much in touching people that he had to eventually have surgery to repair his own tendons! It's my conviction that we can only release healing through love. Faith works by love...here we go again. Love is everything, and if an action is not performed or administered by love, it can't produce an eternal result.

Oh how I love to think of God writing upon my heart! It assures me that when I don't know where to go, He has already programmed it into me to move according to His plan! But it takes knowing Him intimately in order to access the true meaning of His words. You can see this in nature, as I mentioned earlier, but it's good to be reminded that Jesus said this:

"Look at the birds of the air, for they neither sow nor reap nor gather into barns; yet your heavenly Father feeds them. Are you not of more value than they? Which of you by worrying can add one cubit to his stature?"
Mtt 6:22

Okay then, let's examine the bird and reveal the intention of this scripture.

I was studying for a message one Saturday when I came across this truth and was hit by a zenith that changed the scope of my belief about the way God masters everything. Jesus, having been present at whatever type of beginning that preceded from God, knew the intricate details of how everything had been put in a certain order. Even the Chaos in our Solar system has a divine order. When God flung the stars into space or spoke the earth and sky into separation, He had a purpose for everything. The same can be said on the subject of our lives and purposes. And Jesus, knowing our lack of understanding reveals to us in this passage that God programmed into us everything we need to survive. His simple analogy refers to the birds and the lilies in a field.

Here are some things I learned concerning the birds of the air. The sun compass plays a role in homing for the birds and may be used by the ones that migrate during the day. Many songbird species, however, migrate at night. For many years scientist suspected that birds use the stars for navigation. In 1957 Franz and Eleanor Saur collected data from a series of experiments in which birds were placed inside an enclosed planetary dome. The Saurs were able to demonstrate that birds do use the stars for migration but not, as it turns out, in the way they thought. The common belief at the conclusion of the Saur experiments was that birds have a genetically coded map of the stars.

"Emlin, a research scientist, took indigo buntings and put them in a cage so that they could see the sky at night. In the fall the birds kept facing south and in the spring they faced north.

Then he took them into a planetarium. Those large dome-covered buildings house very expensive equipment that is able not only to project points of light where the major stars would be on the sky above, but the equipment can omit various lights. After painstaking work, blotting out certain stars and permitting others to shine, it was learned that the small birds were being navigated by the northern polar stars. This includes Polaris (the north star), the Big and Little Dipper, Cassiopeia, and Cepheus.
In one experiment, he had the north star moved into the western sky, and the birds began facing west. This and similar activities demonstrated the importance of that single star over any other single star in the northern sky.

Then he took a dozen baby indigo buntings, which had never seen the night sky before, and set them out in cages. At first, they did not seem to know directions, but two weeks later, and thereafter, they did. Within two weeks something had matured in their brains and certain inherited knowledge became available to them."

A second theory suggests that birds use the earth's magnetic field to obtain at least a partial map of its position. The earth's magnetic field becomes stronger as you travel away from the equator and toward the poles. In theory, a bird might be able to estimate its latitude based on the strength of the magnetic field. While the change in strength is very small from one location to the next, there is some indication that homing pigeons have the sensitivity to detect even tiny changes in the strength of the magnetic field. Even if true, this would provide only a limited indication of the bird's latitude.

There is some indication that birds use multiple compass methods and calibrate them against each other. Some species use one type of compass as the primary navigational aid while others rely on a different primary system. The complexity of migration and the skill with which it is accomplished is one of the many marvels that make birds so interesting to study.

I'm one who believes that every single word that came from the mouth of Jesus had meaning, not only meaning but life. In other words, the words that took shape from his mouth were and are living organisms themselves. They were said with the intention of either creating, reorganizing or, abolishing evil. In any case they were alive with and for a purpose. And let us note here that the bible clearly states that in the book of Luke when Jesus Himself was making a point for Himself and to the enemy that He spoke this, " It is written, 'Man shall not live by bread alone, but by every Word that proceeds from the mouth of God.'"

The Word "proceeds" written in the Greek translation would indicate an action verb. The Word of God travels and takes on life in itself, creating and forming and bringing about change. Jesus was indicating to satan that it was only by God's Word that things existed and continued to exist. He knew God's Word would ultimately prevail because it's the only truth there is and everything else gravitates around it. The written Word holds concepts, stories, analogies, that all lead to higher truths. And it's these truths that can never cease. Once they left the mouth of God as love, they are on a mission to be fulfilled. That's why it's important to never take the Word of God over your life for granted. I'm not just speaking of the written word which is foundational to every truth that exists. But, God's word is alive and constant and never dies. Once He proclaims a thing over you, it cannot be stopped. Yes, we have the freedom to choose to ignore it, fight it, or accept and embrace it. But God's Word will not return to Him void.

Whatever God's intention may be, is what the nature of His Word takes on. He is forever saying "Let there Be", pronouncing life into anything He designs and intends. The "let there be's" in our lives cannot cease to exist anymore than can light, or the seas, or the fish in the seas, or the fowl of the air. So we can draw hope from this reality, as long as we see the existence of creation, we know the word of the creator continues to "proceed" as alive. By this we take hope that when God formed us in our mother's womb and surely spoke a "let there be" we now are alive. But with that one proclamation he also spawned our purpose, our destiny and our reason for existing. Only in Him will we find these answers. The bible says in Acts 17:28 that "in him" speaking of Christ as the light of truth sent to us, "we live and move and have our being." Wow! We "have" our being. For me, this is where I find my being, my identity. And by that I mean that we must learn through prayer, meditation, and just recognizing the Spirit Jesus left here in order to "have our being"!

I also desire to bring a truth I've come to believe is central to living a life above the fray of everyday expectations and rivalries blocking our way. This scripture exposes the truth of existence...for in Him we do "have" or "possess" our very "being". Now we know that "being" is another word for the properties and characteristics that make us who we are. But it is also an act of existence. In this sense we can speak of the continuing in who we are. In other words we are not in this world to do but to be. If we could put to rest our own aspirations and desires to make something of ourselves we can realize we are already made, now we simply must be.

When observing the actions of the Christ, we see that He postured Himself in a way that appeared to challenge the status quo of His day. Although He instructed His followers to abide by the civil laws, when it came to moral mandates and the present and former Jewish laws He clearly shone a revealing light on the prevailing hypocrisy. His entire quest was to liberate men from their own devises by which they had been bound, well meaning devises in some cases, nonetheless, laws which by nature gave men authority in areas of the societal life which were designed to take away the personal freedoms of humanity that God gifted us with. His attitude far transcended the attitudes of the day where religion resided. He came in, if you will, and turned the soil of man's present condition over and over, as If tilling the ground until the weeds were exposed, weeds that were choking out the true beauty of God's fruits of love.

Although as a basic human race we have come so far in the 2,000 plus years since Jesus, We still find ourselves in a moral dilemma of not understanding that morals cannot be dictated as they must come from an inner source. And that source is what must become more clear and discernible in this present age. As darkness continues to spread through out hearts and minds it is the task of the "enlightened" those who consider themselves to be lined up with Godly intentions for planet earth, to take on a new challenge of becoming more translucent, transparent, and exposed as those who know the source of humanity. And what ever people call "Him", I don't say "it" because I believe this force to be a very personal and intimate creator who is the origin of any type of love...we know Him as God, the force of this entire cosmic condition. If we intend on becoming a pure light to expose evil, cruelty, and oppression of any kind, we must know the one true source of life intimately. The way in which two people not only merge to become one but also to procreate and renew life is represented by the "bed", the place in which we become totally vulnerable and exposed as a lover. We must give our hearts, emotions, and passions to the one who actually created those very elements of life, as a lover, one truly in love, not just in lust, gives themselves over completely to the one who has captivated their thoughts. We must then learn how to hold Him inside after we have spent time communing with Him, either through prayer, mediation, or ingesting His nature by experiencing this earth and all it offers. In our churches as we participate in the partaking of what is liturgically called the

"Eucharist" we celebrate this concept. Rehearsing and doing as Jesus said "in remembrance of Me", which is the eating of the "Lord's supper" and is another way in which we symbolically, or some believe, literally through "transubstantiation", ingest His divinity into our own being. This brings us to our next concept of what must be present in anticipation of a divine visitation.

18 SET THE TABLE

Now we come to the table, and this is so significant to the understanding of how God communes with us. In simplicity, the table is the place that holds the nourishment and nutrients for not only our earthly habitation, our temporary housing, that the Apostle Paul speaks of, but the table is also representative of a place of fellowship, exchanging of thoughts, and even expression. It is at a table where we sit to write out what comes from within our hearts. In the Jewish culture and in many cultures, it is at the table where we can be vulnerable. In bible days if you sat at someone's table it was an act of trust. The disciples routinely ate meals with Jesus, it was an act of intimacy that we really have no comparison to in today's society. At "the last supper", when Jesus revealed the final plan in bringing salvation to mankind, He was met with betrayal. It's never fun to hold a dinner party and have one of your guests ruin the meal because of pettiness or selfishness. But this upper room meal began as any other I'm sure. We can just imagine how the disciples entered kidding with one another, laughing and jesting. They were a brotherhood and only at the table with Jesus or in their private teaching sessions could they let down their guard and truly relax. I love to see families gathering around a table and sharing and swapping stories and laughing. Especially at the Holidays. But this occasion led to more than just full stomachs and relaxed conversation. Jesus takes this time to reveal Himself as the

Savior who would lay down His life. There were various reactions, but none more blatant than Peter's outburst of protest! And then Judas Iscariot is exposed.

So much can happen at a table. Why? first of all there is a captive audience in close proximity. Usually seated close together and facing one another. And together, receiving nourishment that can only come as we vulnerably let go of whatever we are holding in our hands and begin to partake. This is why Jesus so purposefully broke the bread and the wine and told us, many thousands of years later not to forget to do it in our gatherings. Some believe in transubstantiation, which is the belief that the bread and wine become the real Body of Christ once they're blessed. And then there's those who practice communion as a symbolic gesture of partaking and ingesting the Body and the Blood. But however it's done and whatever method is employed to accomplish it, we are dining in the presence of our Lord, and better still being obedient to do as Christ said. When David wrote the following:

"You serve me a six-course dinner right in front of my enemies. You revive my drooping head; my cup brims with blessing."
Psalms 23:5 MSG

He was speaking of that moment we have all experienced when in the middle of great hardship, when we're fighting the enemy within or without, God is there to provide the sustenance we need to survive and beyond. He doesn't give us just enough to get by, no, He feeds us a six course meal! There are many examples of the significance of the table in the bible. I won't take the time to develop them all, but without the table of communion with Him and other believers, and without the table of life where He provides for us, we starve and in no way are capable of being of use to God.

Some diseases that have stolen the lives of many people, especially young people are "Anorexia" and "Bulimia". These diseases ravage the mind and body with the self destructive practices of binging and purging or leading oneself to starvation. I have watched and counseled many young women along the way who would give anything to not be fearful of food. The whole disease is fueled by fear of the lack of control of either the body image we want or an area of life that makes us helpless. The equivalent to this in our Spirit man would be our refusal to take spiritual nourishment. Just as the body has to be fed, so does the spirit in order for it to survive and flourish. And it is our responsibility to make sure we are eating properly, and getting enough, and only you can be the judge of that under the direction of the Holy Spirit. He is our spiritual dietician, if you will, and consulting him on everything we ingest into our spirits makes for a healthy spiritual man!

19 TABLE TEAMWORK

A story in the Old Testament that always touched my heart was the story of Mephibosheth. It is the story of David and his love for Saul's son Jonathan. In 2 Samuel, once David had defeated King Saul and was establishing his own reign, he remembered a promise he had made to Jonathan, a covenant of brotherhood. So, for Jonathan's sake, he rounded up all of Saul's relatives to bless them, yes David blessed his enemy's family. After all was said and done, David asked once again,

"Is there still anyone who is left of the house of Saul, that I may show him kindness for Jonathan's sake?" And the servants told him of Mephibosheth who was lame in his feet. The way I always viewed the story was that this man was ashamed of his inadequacies, the first thing he did in David's presence was to prostrate himself and beg for his life. His exact words were "What is your servant, that you should look upon such a dead dog as I?" A dead dog in the Jewish culture was about as low as it could get. David turned and addressed Saul's top servant Ziba, telling him to continue to work in the fields to feed Saul's sons, but "As for Mephibosheth," said the king, "he shall eat at my table like one of the king's sons."

And it records that he did that for the rest of his days. Another story that is always captivating involves Zacchaeus the tax collector. As Jesus strolled into Nazareth one day doing what

He did, He stopped and noted a man in a tree. The bible notes that this man, Zacchaeus, was short in stature and he wanted to position himself for a better view of this man Jesus who was causing quite a stir. He also happened to be the dreaded tax collector. He was like a cryptic IRS, taking money from the citizens even when they were starving. No one has lost any love for the IRS, but apparently in that day it was worse, tax collectors were looked at as intrusive, taking whatever they wanted from the people to cover their debt to the rulers. But Jesus also saw that this man was also simply a man with a desire to see Him. Zacchaeus probably didn't even know what compelled him to climb up into the tree, but Jesus knew that deep down inside of this man was that desire to see Him. So He calls him down and goes to stay with him and no doubt to eat at his table. Jesus apparently did this often, here's another story denoting his fondness for this element of society.

Jesus found a tax collector named Levi, sitting at the tax office. And He said to him, "Follow Me." So he left all, rose up, and followed Him. Then Levi gave Him a great feast in his own house. And there were a great number of tax collectors and others who sat down with them. And their scribes and the Pharisees complained against His disciples, saying, "Why do you eat and drink with tax collectors and sinners?"
Jesus answered and said to them, " Those who are well have no need of a physician, but those who are sick. I have not come to call the righteous, but sinners, to repentance."

Oh, so now we see His intentions, He was using the table to express the love and acceptance these people had never felt. And as an example to His followers of who He wants at His table. Certainly not the religious, or just the highly educated, but He wants those with the most need! It saddens my heart to say this, but the Church of today walks a fine line between entertaining guests at the table, and feeding those in need. Until we can live a spiritual existence not for ourselves, but for others, God cannot come and grant us His presence. When we spread the table, we must keep an eye out for the needy and sometimes go pull them into share it and we can't expect anything back. These are the sons God is looking for, ones who will open the door and invite everyone in to partake of

God's goodness. That's who we are...once a church loses it's desire or ability to help the needy in soul, spirit and body, it ceases to be an example of Christ Himself.

It's our tendency to categorize people and deliver them into the camp of saint or sinner. There are no such camps in the Kingdom of God. They all sat at the same table as Jesus. These are the ones who need to come eat and drink. If we disagree with an ideology or the way others live their lives, it's not our job to punish them by isolating and excluding them from God's table. People speak of those who "practice wickedness" as people in the bible days spoke of those with leprosy. We somehow think they are contagious and will infect us with their same desires. Good or bad, wicked or righteous, we are all God's people and all the object of his love. Let's read and complete our findings about the table.

20 INSTITUTION OF THE LORD'S SUPPER

"For I received from the Lord that which I also delivered to you: that the Lord Jesus on the same night in which He was betrayed took bread; and when He had given thanks, He broke it and said, 'Take, eat; this is My body which is broken for you; do this in remembrance of Me.' In the same manner He also took the cup after supper, saying, 'This cup is the new covenant in My blood. This do, as often as you drink it, in remembrance of Me.' For as often as you eat this bread and drink this cup, you proclaim the Lord's death till He comes. Therefore whoever eats this bread or drinks this cup of the Lord in an unworthy manner will be guilty of the body and blood of the Lord. But let a man examine himself, and so let him eat of the bread and drink of the cup. For he who eats and drinks in an unworthy manner eats and drinks judgment to himself, not discerning the Lord's body. For this reason many are weak and sick among you, and many sleep. For if we would judge ourselves, we would not be judged. But when we are judged, we are chastened by the Lord, that we may not be condemned with the world. Therefore, my brethren, when you come together to eat, wait for one another. But if anyone is hungry, let him eat at home, lest you come together for judgment"
1 Cor. 11:23-34 NKJV

We, as the sons of God are not here to do God's job for Him.

He will do the separating and dividing! Jesus himself told us that He came to bring a sword to separate the sons from the selfish. We are to do our job, and leave Him to do His. Clearly we are told in this passage that we are to examine ourselves!! We are not told to judge anyone, only to "examine" our own motives and intentions.

That's what God's table is for, to nourish, heal, love and strengthen, and everyone is invited lest we forget that someone invited us. And the last thing we are instructed to do as followers of Jesus in this context of communion is to "tarry" for one another. Or wait for one another and be patient with them, indicating to us God's desire that we, as sons, have an outward focus of love.

Everyone dislikes distasteful people, no one enjoys the person at the party who is there to spoil the fun, the "party pooper" we would call them. Or the guest who was mercifully invited to the dinner and now they have taken the attention from the host to heap the attention upon themselves. There will always be those at the table with us who don't understand who we are to be as sons and daughters of God. They may come and eat at our table and then go tell others how terrible the food was and make fun of our best provisions. But it doesn't matter to God, just like that disrespectful, rebellious child who won't conduct themselves properly at dinner with guests, we are still His children. But we don't decide who makes the cut and who doesn't. Knowing this takes the burden of being judge off of our shoulders, all we're to do is offer ministry, love, teaching, hope, worship, and acceptance and then sit back and let God separate and divide.

Here's all the proof we need:

"And Jesus answered and spoke to them again by parables and said: 'The kingdom of heaven is like a certain king who arranged a marriage for his son, and sent out his servants to call those who were invited to the wedding; and they were not willing to come. Again, he sent out other servants, saying, 'Tell those who are invited, See, I have prepared my dinner; my oxen and fatted cattle are killed, and all things are ready.

Come to the wedding.' But they made light of it and went their ways, one to his own farm, another to his business. And the rest seized his servants, treated them spitefully, and killed them. But when the king heard about it, he was furious. And he sent out his armies, destroyed those murderers, and burned up their city. Then he said to his servants, 'The wedding is ready, but those who were invited were not worthy. Therefore go into the highways, and as many as you find, invite to the wedding.' So those servants went out into the highways and gathered together all whom they found, both bad and good. And the wedding hall was filled with guests. But when the king came in to see the guests, he saw a man there who did not have on a wedding garment. So he said to him, 'Friend, how did you come in here without a wedding garment?' And he was speechless. Then the king said to the servants, 'Bind him hand and foot, take him away, and cast him into outer darkness; there will be weeping and gnashing of teeth."
Mtt. 22:1-13 MSG

Sons must learn to stick to their job and stop sticking their beliefs and proof texts and bible arguments in people's faces. If they are not to be in God's Kingdom for any reason, they will disqualify themselves. It's only ours to stay focused on our Lord and minister back adoration and love to him....

There was one woman dwelling in the city of Bethany and we are told she was even a sinner. While Jesus was sitting at the table this is what she did.

"And being in Bethany at the house of Simon the leper, as He sat at the table, a woman came having an alabaster flask of very costly oil of spikenard. Then she broke the flask and poured it on His head. But there were some who were indignant among themselves, and said, "Why was this fragrant oil wasted? For it might have been sold for more than three hundred denarii and given to the poor." And they criticized her sharply, But Jesus said, " Let her alone. Why do you trouble her? She has done a good work for Me. For you have the poor with you always, and whenever you wish you may do them good; but Me you do not have always. She has done what she could. She has come beforehand to anoint My body for burial.

Assuredly, I say to you, wherever this gospel is preached in the whole world, what this woman has done will also be told as a memorial to her."
Mark 14:3 NKJV

I don't think I need to point out to you the many violations of the Jewish culture and laws that are in this passage. And the violator was none other than the Lord Himself. First He's eating in the house of a filthy leper, breaking a law. Then He allows a woman, another cultural stigma, to anoint Him and minister to Him! I shake my head at times at the gender bias that still exists in the church. When I felt the call to plant a church twenty-two years ago, these biases hit me smack in the face. There were no female senior pastors in our area. I would be the first. There were only two pastors in the whole county, which was very large with many churches, who welcomed me. Even though my husband was with me to "cover" me and I say that from their standpoint, they had a very difficult time accepting me into their "good ole boys" club. One of the kind pastors who had a church right down the street from us, invited me to attend a pastor's luncheon that he hosted monthly, an organization formed to identify the needs of our community and decide how to best address them. When my husband and I hit the door we were met with stares that I was not prepared for. I probably had more experience ministering in my dad's church previously, than most of them had. I had most any educational degree they held but one thing separated us...fear. No one really knew what to say but before we were introduced, I inadvertently over heard one gentleman say, "I didn't know we were suppose to bring our wives". It stung me like salt in a wound because I was so very tired of people accusing me of being where I was because I was someone's daughter, or I was pleasant to look at, or because I was a feminist trying to prove a point. But none of those were true. The truth was I really didn't want to be in a leadership position, particularly as a pastor, and as I looked around the room, I wondered, "how on earth did I get here"? I had that feeling flood over me many times in the years that we had ahead of us. I knew I had to be obedient to what God wanted and at that time He needed for me to help break down some walls. Today there are probably an equal number of men and women pastors in that county. There were other barriers we helped break down. Another one was to awaken the youth of the county and we did just that. None of the things that were accomplished were done by our flesh, they were divinely opened to us. As time went on and God did His work among us, any bias had simply vanished. And thank God we had a wonderful relationship with most every pastor we worked with.

The last and final straw for Jesus' disciples concerned money. "How dare you allow this woman to use this expensive oil on you! We could have used it to help the poor" they said. The Lord's response was surprising when he chided them reminding them that the poor are always needy and always there, but that He would not always be around for them to celebrate with. Money, money, money, what can I say? Not enough, but nothing that hasn't been said. Jesus didn't really have a good relationship with money, not that he minded it, He even tells us to render unto the government what we owe them. But His desire is an attitude and intention. Why do people want money, why are men and women losing marriages and allowing their homes to be exploited and destroyed over money? Yet it happens every day! Money holds a sway over us that we can't resist, it's alluring to the flesh. Commercialism may be our biggest transgression. Money gives a false sense of power and makes one feel that they are untouchable. Even in the church, the wealthy, or those who give the most money, often get the best seats and are given the most honor and are often afforded opportunities not afforded to a nominal tither. But again Jesus made His desire known concerning the use of money in another parable. His strong feelings about it were conveyed in the story of the widow and her two mites. He tells us that her offering was all that she had to her name and she gave it all to the treasury. And although the wealthy gave much, He said she gave more than all the wealthy because they gave out of their surplus and she gave out of her need.

I feel that this story also shows us how when money is richly bestowed upon us and we use it in the correct manner, it is a sweet smelling savor to God, just like that expensive oil was to our Lord.

21 SIT DOWN AND SET A SPELL

I don't really know why my grandparent's generation used this saying, but I remember it. It always made me feel good to hear someone say it. In the south where I was raised we loved sitting outside on a porch swing drinking sweet iced tea (and I mean very sweet), and making slow idle conversation with friends and family. If someone knew you well, they would invite you up to sit with them and serve you sweet tea and maybe something sweet. There was no better feeling! But sitting with someone meant you were willing to invest the time to get to know them and find out about what they had been up to. I guess it was that generation's form of Facebook. A chair says that I want you to sit down, someone has taken the time to prepare a place for you to get off your feet. The chair is very underestimated in its place in making room for God to come into your life. The chair in the Bible symbolizes a place to hold God's glory, it is indicative of royalty such as we find with a throne. The word "chair" is also interchangeable with the word "footstool". This word is used to denote authority, such as "heaven is his throne and earth is his footstool". The footstool holds the weight and glory and is a place to bow at His feet and worship.

"Exalt the Lord our God,
And worship at His footstool— He is holy."
Psalm 95:5

My insight about the provision of the chair is that we are shown that by providing this piece of furniture, the Shunamite woman was expectant of the anointing of the man of God. She was eager to be in the presence of God in the form of His prophet. She was indicating that she totally expected the glory of God to be resting in that room of sacrifice! How do we provide a chair for God's glory, which actually means, God's "weightiness" or His fullness? Who can truly survive being exposed to that level of power? No man can see His glory, and He shares it with no one. But it can rise upon us like the sun rises over the horizon.

"Arise, shine;
For your light has come!
And the glory of the Lord is risen upon you.
For behold, the darkness shall cover the earth, And deep darkness the people;
But the Lord will arise over you,
And His glory will be seen upon you.
The Gentiles shall come to your light,
And kings to the brightness of your rising."
Isaiah 60:1-2

We return here to the very theme of this book that the true sons of God will reflect their Father's glory. Just as a mirror reflects and refracts light, we are placed wherever we may be to reflect His light and shine it wherever God places us in any given moment. His light brightens, heats, exposes, and comforts, it also has healing properties as the laser of God cuts into our hearts with precision and removes any darkness in whatever form it may take. We see the glory of God in Exodus operating as a blazing fire to consume. And a charring fire to burn up the sacrifice, as a cloud and a mist over the people to get their attention. God will work through His sons with precision and power and begin to shine through those who have provided this place for Him. He will do this in His way and His time so that it will make people certain of the origin of the light. The sons will begin to have solutions for the world's various dilemmas. We will begin to not only penetrate different areas of commerce and government, but also move into the areas of science and health. People have been predicting and prophesying this rise of the sons of God for decades probably longer. There have even been groups deceptively using this name to mask and conceal cults. But it's my opinion that the Word of God that I base my findings on shows us the revelation of what is about to come. As the world declines in all areas God is preparing a group of people to step in with answers that not only make sense but that also are shown to be backed with a miraculous divine force. These are they who are getting restless and tired in the traditionally immature church that only knows how to move by what they see and hear, instead of faith in what they know to be true. That truth being that there is another dimension at work at all times. All of our sermons, lessons, songs, praises, worship, good works, and brainy seminars will not bring Him back. Only when this group has been formed, who love as Christ loved, giving portals for divine intervention, can Christ even begin to plan his coming. This is why no man knows the day or the hour because it is set in motion by this group who will be revealed and manifested. And that brings us back to what Paul said.

"All around us we observe a pregnant creation. The difficult times of pain throughout the world are simply birth pangs. But it's not only around us; it's within us. The Spirit of God is arousing us within. We're also feeling the birth pangs. These sterile and barren bodies of ours are yearning for full deliverance. That is why waiting does not diminish us, any more than waiting diminishes a pregnant mother. We are enlarged in the waiting. We, of course, don't see what is enlarging us. But the longer we wait, the larger we become, and the more joyful our expectancy. Meanwhile, the moment we get tired in the waiting, God's Spirit is right alongside helping us along. If we don't know how or what to pray, it doesn't matter. He does our praying in and for us, making prayer out of our wordless sighs, our aching groans. He knows us far better than we know ourselves, knows our pregnant condition, and keeps us present before God. That's why we can be so sure that every detail in our lives of love for God is worked into something good. God knew what He was doing from the very beginning. He decided from the outset to shape

the lives of those who love him along the same lines as the life of His Son. The Son stands first in the line of humanity He restored. We see the original and intended shape of our lives there in Him. After God made that decision of what His children should be like, He followed it up by calling people by name. After He called them by name, He set them on a solid basis with Himself. And then, after getting them established, He stayed with them to the end, gloriously completing what He had begun."
Romans 8:22-30 MSG

How can it be made any clearer for us? We are the time clock for God's movements. Yes, He loves us that much. And He believes in us enough to wait and let us mature into His sons. Part of our responsibility in becoming sons is in our concern over this earth, over other created beings, and for the beauty provided for us, that beauty we are so blatantly destroying one piece at a time. How can we change this? We need to be vigilant in our fight to preserve this good earth. I know it sounds unrealistic but I believe that until the church as a whole begins taking responsibility for their own "carbon footprint", we can never truly be an influence on this world as a whole. Wouldn't it be great if church campuses would strive to be self reliant for energy and other natural resources? What an example we could set as God gave us wisdom on how to make better use of the provisions He has given us. We are to be stewards over this earth. Have you ever taken the time to understand the responsibility given to us by God? The definition that Mr. Webster gives is very close to the definition of the word in Greek in the New Testament.

Steward: a person who manages another's property or financial affairs; one who administers anything as the agent of another or others.

What does it say that God, the very Author of creation, would give us, as mere mortals, the responsibility for the care of the earth? I am not a political person, however, I am in a process of "becoming" a son of God and in that regard, I will support whatever is best for this earth. Of course when Jesus returns there will be a New Heaven and A New Earth! I have no idea what that will look like, but if we have accomplished our task of bringing our environment back under submission to God, it will be a garden of unimaginable beauty!

So pull up a chair and let's open ourselves for more of God's weightiness, we can handle it, He created us to hold His glory, in fact it's already deposited there in each of us just waiting to be released!

22 TURN ON THE LAMP PLEASE

"This is the crisis we're in: God–light streamed into the world, but men and women everywhere ran for the darkness. They went for the darkness because they were not really interested in pleasing God. Everyone who makes a practice of doing evil, addicted to denial and illusion, hates God–light and won't come near it, fearing a painful exposure. But anyone working and living in truth and reality welcomes God–light so the work can be seen for the God–work it is."
John 3:19-21 MSG

I love the term "God-light", it's indicative of that eternal light that fuels heaven and provides everything we need. One thing that I take close interest in as a builder's wife, is the accessories in a house. The accessories are those pieces that are not necessarily furniture, but those things strategically placed to bring the most desirable effect. They may have no function except to bring more attention and beauty to the room, but they are nonetheless important. I have explained to my husband Wes time and again that if he wants to impress a woman looking for a house, he needs to stage the room to look warm and comfortable. A room, depending on it's function, should be inviting and comfortable, as well as beautiful. And the most important thing in making a house warm is the use of lamps. I understand that for functionality, especially in a kitchen, the best lighting is overhead fluorescents. But the light cast by the fluorescent bulb is just not warm, and I hate to admit it, but I don't like that much light. So in addition to the overheads we usually use pendants. But the family room, or living room, or whatever you call it is so much more inviting in the lamp light. And I don't want lamps that are just functional, but with a certain color shade so that they cast the right kind of light.

I have a confession to make of something I've done since I was a little girl, when I'm riding in a car at night, in the passenger's seat, I will often peek into the houses along the way to see what kind of lighting they use and whether or not I could live with it. Now we're usually going way too fast for me to see much more than that! Especially with my husband driving! But I like inviting homes and I enjoy imagining what goes on behind the windows. A Voyeur I'm not, but if I could really see into those homes I would probably be disappointed. In my imagination there are always loving families gathered around dinner tables sharing and laughing. But to me, a lower lamp light is much more conducive to relaxation. In my house we use only lamps in the evenings to read by and watch television. And this brings us to the next item that was provided for the prophet, the lamp. The obvious significance here is that a lamp sheds light upon all of our activities, sparing none. Yes, we know that Jesus is the light of the world but we also know that there was a time before light. Genesis says that God spoke and said "let there be light"! Before this proclamation of creation, the Spirit of The Lord was hovering over the face of the deep, brooding and cultivating for what was coming. It interests me that we're told in Genesis that the earth was without form and void and that darkness covered the face of the deep. So darkness was either already present or a result and fulfillment of the law in the Universe of opposites. This law is about seeing the two sides to everything...the positive side and the negative side. In whatever way the darkness began it's existence, God looked at the light and thought it was good. From that time forth God inhabited the light.

When we speak of this last necessity that was given to provide a room for the prophet, we come to the most important aspect of "becoming" a son of God, Because now we are gaining insight into the one who already blazed a path for us to follow. He was and is the everlasting "stereotype" in this sense: " Noun meaning "a stereotype plate" is from 1817. Meaning "image perpetuated without change". God gave us His son as the God image so that we can be hammered into His image by the blacksmith and come out as a duplicate. We are to be melted, poured, molded, and come out made in His likeness. And it's the circumstances that set up around us that can help work us into that perfect image.

The "lamp stand" or the "candlestick" is representative of Jesus Christ among us. What a beautiful picture we see here. And it's necessary that we know who He is. Only when we have a personal revelation of Him, can we even begin to "become" a son. And it's a personal requirement because you and I, all of us, must have that personal insight into Him. A popular trend taking place in some churches today teaches that we are all saved by grace, not necessarily through Christ, the sacrificial Lamb. They teach that any channel a seeker may access, as long as it leads towards the nature of Christ is equivalent to and just as redemptive as the plan of Salvation through our Lord Jesus Christ. As wonderful as this feels to believe, that everyone will wind up in the same place with God in the end, it's improbable and actually goes against the laws of the Universe. However, I would not presume to think God couldn't do anything He wanted to do, the way He wanted to do it! We are all His children but if there is no freedom of choice when it comes to our eternal estate, then God has broken His own intention of making man in His image with free will. So the lamp most definitely needs to be set up and turned on for God's presence to dwell with His people. I think it's time we lift Jesus up in our churches. It's no longer about forms, liturgy, or episcopal structure, in our worship, time is critical, we don't have time to waste performing practices in our churches that should have been put away long ago. We must put a stop to our arguing and bickering about what is true and do the one thing we know is right, gather around that lamp stand, Jesus Christ, putting Him in the center of all we do. For He is the way, the truth, and the life. The whole world is in a pregnant condition waiting for us to truly become Christ, setting in motion the return and victory of our Lord Jesus Christ over darkness everywhere. And anyone who tries to enter His Kingdom by any other door will fail.

23 THE ROOM IS READY

One of the main joys of my life is being a grandmother. There are no words to express the love and affection I feel for my grandchildren. I always have a room that they can call their own so they feel comfortable at Grandbee and Papa's house because I realize that there is no comfort like having your own drawer in which to put your belongings. My husband has to share the closet space in this bedroom because my closet is full and if he could hang his clothes there, he probably would have a hard time having them handy to pull on as he always does. It's just easier for him to have his own space and he likes it that way. But on recent visits to my house my grandchildren have brought his disorganization to my attention. Especially my granddaughter who is truly bothered by the fact that our clothes don't hang together. It's a big deal for her! So when we know the kids are coming over we make haste to prepare the room!! My husband so ever kindly goes in and straightens out his things and puts as much of it out of sight as possible. And to these children, it a very special thing that he respects that it is also their room. We make them feel welcome by preparing a place for them to be comfortable.

It's the same principle we employ when making a room for the presence of God. My encouragement is simply for us to sit back and reexamine where we are personally in this quest. Would God have a place with you? Would he feel comfortable in your home? If not, are you now willing to begin the preparations to have Him come and abide with you, showing you how to be His son?

It's time for those who call themselves "Christ followers" and "children of God" to grow up. Jesus desires to come find a people as His Bride ready to dwell in Him and Him in them. He needs us, yes, He does need us to fulfill this plan of redemption that was set in motion from the beginning of creation.

It's my intention in writing this book to provoke us to thought and awaken within each reader the same desire I have, which is to lay down all pretenses and simply "Be", little images of Him in all we do, thus bringing redemption and in so doing help bring the culmination of the ages. I am giving you a heads up to go now and fill your lamps so you won't be turned away.

"God's kingdom is like ten young virgins who took oil lamps and went out to greet the bridegroom. Five were silly and five were smart. The silly virgins took lamps, but no extra oil. The smart virgins took jars of oil to feed their lamps. The bridegroom didn't show up when they expected him, and they all fell asleep. In the middle of the night someone yelled out, 'He's here! The bridegroom's here! Go out and greet him!'
"The ten virgins got up and got their lamps ready. The silly virgins said to the smart ones, 'Our lamps are going out; lend us some of your oil.'"They answered, 'There might not be enough to go around; go buy your own.' They did, but while they were out buying oil, the bridegroom arrived. When everyone who was there to greet him had gone into the wedding feast, the door was locked. Much later, the other virgins, the silly ones, showed up and knocked on the door, saying, 'Master, we're here. Let us in. He answered, 'Do I know you? I don't think I know you. So stay alert. You have no idea when he might arrive."
Matthew 25:1-13 MSG

24 EMBRACE YOUR PROMISE

Now let's take our story of the Shunammite woman and find out the end of the story, the culmination of your obedience...

"One day Elisha passed through Shunem. A leading lady of the town talked him into stopping for a meal. And then it became his custom: Whenever he passed through, he stopped by for a meal."I'm certain," said the woman to her husband, "that this man who stops by with us all the time is a holy man of God. Why don't we add on a small room upstairs and furnish it with a bed and desk, chair and lamp, so that when he comes by he can stay with us?" And so it happened that the next time Elisha came by he went to the room and lay down for a nap. Then he said to his servant Gehazi, "Tell the Shunammite woman I want to see her." He called her and she came to him. Through Gehazi Elisha said, "You've gone far beyond the call of duty in taking care of us; what can we do for you? Do you have a request we can bring to the king or to the commander of the army?" She replied, "Nothing. I'm secure and satisfied in my family." Elisha conferred with Gehazi: "There's got to be something we can do for her. But what?" Gehazi said, "Well, she has no son, and her husband is an old man." "Call her in," said Elisha. He called her and she stood at the open door. Elisha said to her, "This time next year you're going to be nursing an infant son" "O my master, O Holy Man," she said, "don't play games with me, teasing me with such

fantasies!" The woman conceived a year later, just as Elisha had said, she had a son. The child grew up. One day he went to his father, who was working with the harvest hands, complaining, "My head, my head!" His father ordered a servant, "Carry him to his mother." The servant took him in his arms and carried him to his mother. He lay on her lap until noon and died. She took him up and laid him on the bed of the man of God, shut him in alone, and left. She then called her husband, "Get me a servant and a donkey so I can go to the Holy Man; I'll be back as soon as I can." "But why today? This isn't a holy day—it's neither New Moon nor Sabbath." She said, "Don't ask questions; I need to go right now. Trust me." She went ahead and saddled the donkey, ordering her servant, "Take the lead—and go as fast as you can; I'll tell you if you're going too fast." And so off she went. She came to the Holy Man at Mount Carmel.The Holy Man, spotting her while she was still a long way off, said to his servant Gehazi, "Look out there; why, it's the Shunammite woman! Quickly now, Ask her, 'Is something wrong? Are you all right? Your husband? Your child?' "She said, "Everything's fine." But when she reached the Holy Man at the mountain, she threw herself at his feet and held tightly to him. Gehazi came up to pull her away, but the Holy Man said, "Leave her alone—can't you see that she's in distress? But God hasn't let me in on why; I'm completely in the dark." Then she spoke up: "Did I ask for a son, master? Didn't I tell you, 'Don't tease me with false hopes'?" He ordered Gehazi, "Don't lose a minute—grab my staff and run as fast as you can. If you meet anyone, don't even take time to greet him, and if anyone greets you, don't even answer. Lay my staff across the boy's face." The boy's mother said, "As sure as God lives and you live, you're not leaving me behind." And so Gehazi let her take the lead, and followed behind? But Gehazi arrived first and laid the staff across the boy's face. But there was no sound—no sign of life. Gehazi went back to meet Elisha and said, "The boy hasn't stirred." Elisha entered the house and found the boy stretched out on the bed dead. He went into the room and locked the door—just the two of them in the room—and prayed to God. He then got into bed with the boy and covered him with his body, mouth on mouth, eyes on eyes, hands on hands. As he was stretched out over him. He then got into bed with the boy

and covered him with his body, mouth on mouth, eyes on eyes, hands on hands. As he was stretched out over him like that, the boy's body became warm. Elisha got up and paced back and forth in the room. Then he went back and stretched himself upon the boy again. The boy started sneezing—seven times he sneezed!—and opened his eyes. He called Gehazi and said, "Get the Shunammite woman in here!" He called her and she came in. Elisha said, "Embrace your son!"
2 Kings 4:8-36 MSG

What a way to end this amazing depiction of God's grace. If we make a place for Him and keep it prepared, He will come and nap, and sit with us and even desire to know our hearts and our biggest desires! The prophet didn't even wait for this woman to ask for anything, he offered to answer whatever request she had. Isn't it great when we find ourselves in the season of unexpected blessings? We are blessed daily with new mercies, forgiveness, breath, health, anything good comes as a blessing, and they're usually taken for granted. But when those things come out of God's extravagant love that sneak up and surprise us, we are overjoyed. Did we ever doubt that God was able? Did we doubt that He hears our every whisper? We shouldn't because all He's waiting for is the right time and season! And this was the case with this noble woman, she didn't even have to ask. If we want more of that kind of blessing, we have to make a conscious effort to make a place for the one who bestows the blessing.

The most calming thing to remember in this life is, "the Lord giveth and The Lord take the away"! It always seems that when God brings people into a time of unexpected blessing the first thing we want to say is, "it's about time"! Our gratitude level seems extremely hollow, and we even begin taking it for granted with the expectation that that's exactly how we should be treated, that's human nature. The danger is, the blessing can become the curse if we don't know how to handle it, because we turn on our Father, who is our only hope.

The progression of this story is predictable in that sense for several reasons. First, when God blesses us and gives a provision, it's always Satan's job to either kill, steal, or destroy it and he doesn't let up! In this instance the enemy decided to go all out and kill the child stealing his life and the joys of motherhood from this lady. And following suit with how humanity traditionally looks at God as a big force in the sky doling out blessings and cursings as He wills, she needed to blame the prophet. Grabbing him by his feet, she implores him to listen, and then she accuses him of being deceptive about the fulfilled promise. How many times have I found myself here?? I can't even tell you! "God, you promised you'd keep us from harm and danger, why didn't you?", or "you promised you'd provide for me if I did this, where are you?" But there's one very important phrase in here that we overlook. "She took him and laid him on the bed of the man of God". What does this say about her? Well, she knew her source and had she not made a place for the source to dwell with her she wouldn't have had the confidence to believe for a miracle. She was willing to let it go, and she knew who to give it to! Ultimately the prophet leaves what he's attending to and personally takes care of the miracle, bringing the boy back to life. And he says "woman embrace your son." Oh wow! I would like to think that our faith in making a place for God as this book has taught us would evoke that kind of response from God's Holy Spirit. I want to hear Him finally say, "here it is daughter, your promise, healed, sealed and delivered into your embrace.

I pray now that these writings have penetrated your heart and captured your mind so that you might begin that building process, I pray that your every desire comes to you in God's season, knowing that His timing is the best. And I pray that you too will hear those words that bring hope! "Son or daughter embrace your promise"!

Conclusion:
To be or not to be
My whole purpose for writing this is an attempt to stir us into action as the Sons of God. The Day of The Lord is drawing nigh and I can feel Ezekial's bones shaking. It's only in the dry valley where resurrection can occur so miraculously. I hope this gets us started. I foresee those who will step forth in leadership to help mobilize this army.

The last thought I will leave you with is the most valuable so don't miss it! God didn't make us to "do", He made us to "be" someone, He made us to live an abundant life. He didn't make us to always be striving with religion and methods, all you and I need to do is just "be". Be the best we can be right where we are under the guidance of God's spirit who resides with us. Be a child of God a true son! So please, after all is said and done, my last words will be, just be who you are! Don't try so hard, it doesn't take a whole lot of striving to just relax and be. So breathe, inhale, exhale, and say "I am all God wants me to be". Now here comes your future!

ABOUT THE AUTHOR

Beth Bonner has been a Pastor for 24 years. Traveling in her early days to help host Christian television programming for an international ministry. Beth and her husband began a church in 1992 which they co-pastored for 16 years. Beth has been married for 36 years and has 2 children and 4 grandchildren. Having grown up in a pastor's home Beth examines the church and its inner workings from her personal experiences. Beth now writes from home and accepts outside speaking engagements.

Beth can be contacted at: romabeth1@gmail.com

Made in the USA
Charleston, SC
09 March 2014